THE ROMAN REPUBLIC

SUTTON POCKET HISTORIES

THE ROMAN REPUBLIC

ANDREW LINTOTT

SUTTON PUBLISHING

First published in the United Kingdom in 2000 by
Sutton Publishing Limited · Phoenix Mill
Thrupp · Stroud · Gloucestershire · GL5 2BU

British Library Cataloguing in Publication Data
A catalogue record for this book is available from the British
Library.

ISBN 0-7509-2223-0

Typeset in 11/16 pt Baskerville.
Typesetting and origination by
Sutton Publishing Limited.
Printed in Great Britain by
Cox & Wyman, Reading, Berkshire.

Contents

List of Dates

280–275	War with Pyrrhus, King of Epirus, and south Italian alliance.
272	Capture of Tarentum. Livius Andronicus taken to Rome.
264–241	First Punic War. Rome gets control of Sicily from Carthaginians.
241–238	Carthaginian mercenary war, ending with surrender of Sardinia to Rome.
232–218	Wars with Gauls. Occupation of Gallic territory on Adriatic and in Cisalpine Gaul.
229–228	First Illyrian War.
225	Ebro agreement between Rome and Hasdroubal.
219	Second Illyrian War.
218–202	Second Punic War. Battles of Trasimene (217), Cannae (216), Metarurus (207) and Zama (202). Rome seizes Spain and demilitarises Carthage.
215–206	First Macedonian War.
c. **200**	First Roman histories written by Fabius Pictor and Cincius Alimentus in Greek.
200–197	Second Macedonian War (Cynoscephalai 197).
196	Flamininus' declaration of the freedom of Greece.
192–189	War with Antiochus the Great.
184	Censorship of Cato.
171–168	Third Macedonian and Illyrian Wars.
149–146	Third Punic War, ending in destruction of Carthage. Africa becomes a province.

149–147	Andriscus' revolt in Macedon suppressed. Macedonia becomes a province.
147–146	War with Achaean League ending in destruction of Corinth.
137–133 **(and 104–1)**	Slave revolts in Sicily.
134	Capture of Numantia ends Viriathic War in Spain.
133	Tribunate of Tiberius Gracchus. Land bill. Kingdom of Pergamum left to Rome (becomes a province, called Asia).
125	Fulvius Flaccus proposes citizenship for Latins and Italians. Revolt of Fregellae.
124 –118	War in Transalpine Gaul. New province created. Foundation of Narbo.
123–122	Tribunates of Gaius Gracchus. Land bill, grain bill, reform of courts, attempt to found Junonia on site of Carthage, unsuccessful bill to give citizenship to Latins.
111–105	War against Jugurtha in Africa.
107, 104–100	Marius six times consul. Military reforms (104) lead to defeats of Teutones and Cimbri in 102 (Aquae Sextiae) and 101 (Vercellae).
106	Births of Cicero and Pompey.
101	Servilius Glaucia tribune. Victory over pirates. Cilicia becomes a province.
100	Saturninus tribune. Popular legislation and violence. Deaths of Saturninus and Glaucia. Birth of C. Iulius Caesar.

91	Tribunate of Livius Drusus. Bills about land, grain and the courts. Failure of Italian bill leads to outbreak of 'Social War'. Italian confederation.
90	Roman citizenship for Latins and Italians conceded in principle.
89	Capture of Asculum by Romans. End of Italian confederation. Mithridates invades western Asia Minor.
88	Sulla consul; Sulpicius tribune. Quarrel over Italian proposals and Mithridatic command leads to violence and Sulla's march on Rome. Mithridates' forces reach Greece.
87–84	Sulla in East (settlement with Mithridates 85). Supporters of Marius take over in Rome.
83–82	Renewed civil war. Sulla victorious in Italy.
81	Sulla's dictatorship and constitutional reforms. Proscriptions.
79–72	Sertorian revolt in Spain.
74 onwards	New Mithridatic War. Lucullus victorious in Bithynia (73) and Pontus (72–1). Lucullus pursues Mithridates into Armenia.
73–71	Revolt of gladiators, slaves and free herdsmen in south Italy under Spartacus.
70	Consulship of Pompey and Crassus. Powers removed by Sulla restored to tribunes. Trial of Verres. Birth of Vergil.
67	Pompey suppresses piracy.

Map of the Italian peninsula.

Map of Rome and its environs.

ONE

The Emergence of Rome

At the beginning of the Republic, in about 500 BC, Rome was a city on the eastern bank of the Tiber with a civic nucleus centring on the marshy ground by the river and settlements spreading over the surrounding tufa hills. Its area was large for those times, but not densely populated. The city's land lay mainly to the east of the Tiber, extending not much more than 15 miles in any direction from the centre of the city. In this direction Rome was hemmed in by her Latin allies and neighbours – cities such as Tibur (Tivoli), Praeneste (Palestrina), Tusculum and Aricia.

The Latins were a branch of the Italic peoples sharing a language, religious cults, some legal traditions, and a military organisation that could be used to fight wars against common enemies. Rome's neighbours west of the Tiber were the Etruscans, a loosely connected league of warlike, prosperous and cultured city dwellers, who spoke a language unrelated to those of other Italians. They had an impact on Rome that matched that of her Latin kinsfolk. There were also, in a circle from the north to the south-east of Latium, a variety of Italic peoples, living mainly in the Apennines – Volscians, Aequians, Umbrians, Sabines, Marsians, Samnites and others. Their connection with Rome was more remote, except for the Sabines who were held to have contributed to the ethnic mixture of the city. Their languages are normally classified as branches of Oscan (Umbrian forming a particularly distinct variety). Though at first sight strikingly different in appearance, these have a similar structure to Latin and share some vocabulary: they can be translated into Latin word for word.

Significant visitors had come to Italy from abroad: Greeks had settled in colonies in the south and had a trading post at Graviscae in Etruria (their influence can be detected in early Rome). Carthaginians were more transient, but we are told that their earliest treaty with Rome dated from the beginning of the Republic, and their presence is clear in a bilingual Etruscan and Punic dedication at a shrine to Astarte at Pyrgi on the Etruscan coast.

The early Roman economy was founded on agriculture: Rome had no iron workings such as the Etruscans possessed nor any source of outstanding building material. Although peninsular Italy is dominated by the mountain chain of the Apennines, there are, apart from coastal valleys and fertile upland basins, two major plains to the west, those of Latium and Campania. The western coastline has, moreover, a much higher rainfall overall than that of the Adriatic shore. Rome possessed both a river crossing and a river port, with a further port nearer the Tiber's mouth at Ostia. Though economic necessity did not force Rome to look overseas for prosperity, and it was a long time before Rome turned to maritime conquest, the city was open to overseas goods and influences from long before the beginning of the Republic.

Before the Republic there had been kings. According to later Roman historians these were seven, including the founding father Romulus. Ancient chronographic juggling gave Rome a foundation date in the middle of the eighth century BC. However, archaeology has revealed settlements on the hills of Rome as far back as the Bronze Age, followed by Iron Age settlement in villages of huts (their form preserved by the surviving cremation urns), which stretches back beyond 900 BC. From about 700 BC we find an expansion in habitation and the economy with evidence of a luxurious warrior aristocracy. Then, towards the end of the seventh century, the Forum area was drained and paved, and during the following century Rome acquired the temples and other public structures that characterised an ancient city state. Roman historians placed here the reigns of two Etruscan kings and the husband of an Etruscan princess. Etruscan writers, by contrast, saw Rome falling into the hands of Etruscan warlords. The Romans inherited from Etruria items of political ritual and paraphernalia – the *fasces* (the bundles of rods round an axe pertaining to senior magistrates), the ritual of a military triumph, the practice of augury, i.e. the search for portents in the natural world, especially in the flight of birds or the entrails of sacrificed animals – although how deep their influence was on other features of Roman society is another matter.

Serious doubts have been expressed about Roman historical tradition. It was only in the third century BC that literature began to emerge in Rome, beginning with epic and drama, following the example of the Greeks. Roman histories were not composed before about 200 BC, and these were originally in Greek, not Latin (although this was already used for historical epic). However, writing in Latin is found from the regal period onwards on stone, bronze and ceramics. The question is, what sort of material could the earliest Roman historians use when they came to reconstruct early Roman history.

The central component was the Fasti. This was at first the term for the calendar of days proper for public and private business, announced every month by the priesthood called pontiffs (*pontifices*). It was then transferred to the list of years from the beginning of the Republic, each designated by the names of the two consuls (there was no dating from the foundation of the city until a historical consensus emerged at the end of the Republic as to when that was). The pontiffs in due course added to their records of consular names odd notes of significant events, such as wars, famines and religious portents, that happened in each respective year: these records were called the annals (*annales*) of the pontiffs and this name was also applied later to histories of Rome that recorded events year by year. There was no systematic edition of the annals of the pontiffs until the late Republic, well after the emergence of annals written by historians, and it is hard to judge their value beyond that of providing a list of consular names. In view of variant traditions and the doubts of Romans themselves, the reliability of even this list is questionable for the first two centuries of the Republic.

What other material was available? First, there were the records of aristocratic families. Of these a small fraction survives to us directly in the epitaphs on tombs, dating back to about 300 BC, but much more was known to Roman annalists, thanks to the Roman practice of elaborate funeral eulogies delivered in public in the forum, paying tribute not only to the dead man but his ancestors. However, these were notorious for their corruption through aristocratic rivalry. We also hear of songs about famous men sung at dinners, and there is evidence of historical wall paintings. Secondly, it is likely that the plebs kept records of their own magistrates and major events in their struggle with the patrician aristocracy in the early Republic. Thirdly, the various priesthoods recorded events of religious importance. Beyond this, Greek writers related events of international significance, such as the sack of Rome by Gauls in the early fourth century, while the colonies founded by Rome would have remembered the dates and details of their own origins. Finally, there remained embedded in the Roman political and religious system of the middle Republic evidence for its past history.

Nevertheless, the history of the early Republic must contain, and must always have contained, a great deal of conjecture, and this is even more true of the regal period, once we move beyond the basic archaeological record. What can be reasonably said about the city in which a republic was to be created? It was certainly ruled by kings, who were the centre of an aristocracy. The aristocracy probably already had formal meetings in a senate and there may well have been some sort of popular assemblies that listened and expressed approval or indignation at what their betters had decided. The clans (*gentes*) in which the aristocracy was distributed were also important. Some had the supervision of religious cults, others gave their name to some of the territorial divisions into which the citizen body was divided. It is not clear whether the proletariat was all assigned to these clans or had some subordinate relation to them. However, the institution of patrons and clients had an ancient origin, and this simultaneously provided a means of protection for the weak and a combination of physical assistance and prestige for the powerful.

The territorial expansion of the city presupposes military strength. Warriors in armour resembling that of the Greek heavily armed soldier (*hoplite*) are depicted on terracotta friezes in Latium from the regal period. Roman annalists ascribe to the last king but one, Servius Tullius, a reform whereby the citizens were classified according to wealth and military function in a census and this was the basis of both recruitment and membership of a political assembly. The bulk of the army and the assembly were infantry, with the cavalry assigned a prestigious position of seniority. Even if the details of this reform are insecure, it is plausible to ascribe Rome's relative strength in about 500 BC to the grant of full citizen status to her infantry.

A visitor to Rome at the end of the sixth century BC would have found an early version of the Forum Romanum – no stone paving, but a drained and levelled area, surrounded no doubt by wooden shops. At the north-west end there was a small assembly area next to a shrine of Vulcan, at the south-east end the headquarters of the king (Regia) and the Temple of Vesta, where the eternal fire of the city burned. Beyond this, on the north-eastern slope of the Palatine hill were aristocrats' houses raised in timber on lower courses of massive ashlar stone blocks, whose focus on a central atrium shows them to be the ancestors of the traditional Roman house. To the west, by the river, there were the cattle and vegetable markets, the former graced by a spectacular temple dedicated to Fortuna and Mater Matuta. This was made of timber on a stone base with terracotta decoration, like other Latin and Etruscan temples of the period. A terracotta frieze showed chariots pulled by sphinxes; a pediment portrayed Athena with Hercules. Above this towered the Capitol with the new temple to Jupiter Capitolinus, larger but constructed in the same fashion as that below it. Beyond the Capitol and outside the boundary of the city proper lay the Field of Mars (Campus Martius), at this point an open space where the army enrolled and drilled and where the military assembly met.

Little can be safely said of the culture of the period. Some people were literate, but writing was used wholly or mainly for utilitarian ends. There was no native coinage as there was in the Greek world at the time, weighed bronze being used as a conveyance of value. The influence of the visual arts of Greece and the East could be seen, equally the impact of their religions. However, the calendar was dominated by the festivals of Roman or Italic cults, which, unlike their Greek counterparts, were not associated with myth and whose underlying principles were often impenetrable to later generations of Romans. Some cults were shared with the Latins, including the cult of Diana on the Aventine hill south of the city, the cults at Lavinium (later famed for its association with Aeneas), and that of Jupiter Latiaris in the Alban hills to the south of Latium. The principal rite of this last cult was called the Latin festival and held in spring. Most of the inhabitants of Rome then left the city for the Alban hills, where a major celebration occurred before the start of the campaigning season.

Rome's relations with her Latin kinsfolk then were intense in spite of rivalries between cities. We should probably regard later elements of the 'law of Latium' as natural products of this period – the right of intermarriage, the right to own land in the territory of a different Latin city, the right to migrate or to go into exile in another Latin city. In the early Republic Rome was to co-operate with her neighbours in the founding of colonies in order to provide new land for cultivation and secure the defence of Latium.

At the end of the sixth century Etruscan influence in Latium was strong and resented. The Latins used the aid of Aristodemos, the tyrant of Greek Cumae, to defeat the Etruscans at Aricia in 505. This breakdown of Etruscan power occurred within a few years of the date the Romans later calculated for the expulsion of their last Etruscan king, Tarquin the Proud. It is likely that they were connected. At all events, Latium became free and Rome, after some vicissitudes (Etruscan historians maintained that Lars Porsenna actually gained possession of Rome and had to be bought off), became a republic.

TWO

Early Political Struggles

The story of the early Republic in our sources has two elements: wars against hostile neighbours – for the most part the hillmen (Volsci, Aequi, Hernici) but also the Etruscans – and a vigorous domestic struggle at home. It should be said that for the fifth century BC the evidence of archaeology fails us; we have almost nothing, whether building or artefact, that attests this period, and one may be tempted to conclude that this was in fact a period of considerable poverty and weakness. The reliability of the tradition about the wars of the fifth century is almost completely in doubt, except perhaps the founding of early colonies as a protection for Latium and a source of new land. The story of the conflict at home may be questioned in detail, but its general theme is borne out by its product, the peculiar constitution of the Roman Republic. Polybius, the Greek historian who recorded in the second century BC Rome's rise to dominion over the Mediterranean lands, argued that this mixture of monarchy, oligarchy and democracy was not, like other similar constitutions, the deliberate creation of a law-giver but the product of a natural evolution, in which the elements were in creative conflict with one another. His view was based on the story of these early political struggles.

The Romans believed that the expulsion of Tarquin the Proud was a violent reaction to the high-handed behaviour of the king and his family. In consequence the title of *rex* was accursed under the Republic, only being permitted to one religious official, and people who behaved like kings were liable to be killed on sight. The aristocracy arranged for the election by the people of two of their number to hold the equivalent of regal power, symbolised in the *fasces*, for only one year at a time. These were the consuls, who gave their names to their year of office, were the supreme military commanders and oversaw administration at home. Their election took place in the military assembly (the *comitia centuriata*), where preponderance of votes was in the hands of the cavalry and wealthier infantrymen. The aristocratic council of the senate became more important, and the aristocracy sought to divide itself from the rest of the people as a privileged group, the patricians. This led to protest by the masses outside, the plebeians. Their grievances, we are told, concerned the allocation of the public land, won in wars, and the treatment of debtors. It was the latter in particular that caused the plebs (in 494) to leave the city in a 'secession' – either to the Aventine hill just south of the city or to the Sacred Hill to the north-east – so depriving the aristocracy of much of its military manpower. The aristocracy decided to negotiate with representatives elected by the plebs, its first tribunes (*tribuni plebis*). These people were declared sacrosanct by the plebs, that is, a physical violation of their persons was to be treated as a capital offence and avenged by any member of the plebs without further prompting.

In consequence, although there was as yet no long-term change in the treatment of debt and public land, the tribunes and their status were recognised. Moreover, it was accepted that the tribunes might employ their sacrosanct persons in defence of any plebeian who enlisted their aid against a magistrate threatening arbitrary punishment or a powerful private citizen, such as a creditor, threatening force.

This was linked with the custom of citizens crying for help to their fellows (*provocatio*), when confronted with the authority of magistrates. The secession thus created the basis of personal liberty for the ordinary Roman. It also was the origin of one of the most remarkable magistracies of all time. Tribunes came to interpose their sacrosanct persons not only to protect individuals but to disrupt and veto acts of public business (*intercessio*). They held meetings of the plebs, called *concilia*, which discussed matters, passed resolutions (*plebiscita*) and even held unofficial trials of the plebs' enemies. The number of tribunes grew to ten and two assistants (*aediles plebis*) were also elected.

What modern historians call the Conflict of the Orders was to continue for over two more centuries. During this period the divide between patricians and plebeians was almost reduced to insignificance, some genuine relief was given over debt and land distribution, and the republican constitution was vastly elaborated. It was not a story of unbroken plebeian success. After long agitation over the need for a written law-code, a commission of ten was appointed to draft one (451–450). In its second year, the job done, the commission refused to abdicate and was only deposed after another secession. The new law-code, the Twelve Tables, seems to have largely dealt with private law, but, though recognising *provocatio*, it circumscribed the plebs in other ways and in particular introduced a ban on intermarriage between patricians and plebeians which was repealed shortly afterwards. The aristocracy was tenacious and largely united. When certain people rose to popularity by relieving popular economic distress, they were regarded as incipient tyrants and killed, with or without legal pretext. Demagogues were objects of suspicion.

During the early Republic new magistracies were created: quaestors to be assistants to the consuls with special responsibility for finance: censors to count the Roman citizen body and assess its wealth; and the dictator, in origin a short-term magistracy, which united the powers of the consuls in a single command to deal with an emergency, usually military. Plebeians were rarely, if ever, elected to the major magistracies. In about 400 BC a compromise was in operation, whereby consuls were not usually elected but tribunes of the soldiers with consular power, a more numerous magistracy open to plebeians. Eventually, a pair of tribunes, Licinius and Sextius, successfully combined pressure over the opening of the consulship to the plebeians with agitation over the distribution of public land. At first one plebeian consul was permitted, and a ceiling was put on the use of public land for agriculture or grazing by a single individual (in 367). A new magistrate, called praetor, was created to assist the consuls, and 'curule' aediles were elected by the whole people to share with their plebeian counterparts the task of supervising the fabric and the non-political activities of the city itself.

In the century that followed plebeians were granted an exclusive right to one of the consulships and an option on the other (in 342). The other magistracies of the people were soon opened to them; so too were half the major priesthoods (in 300) – that is, the *pontifices* (whose president, the *pontifex maximus*, had general oversight of the priesthoods and public religion) and the augurs (*augures*), the experts in divination. In the same year the popular self-defence of *provocatio* received some legal reinforcement. Meanwhile, some regulation was introduced to the membership of the senate by making it the responsibility of the censors. It must be assumed that priests and former senior magistrates, who were plebeian, were now members. Tribunes were not members but were allowed to sit in at meetings. A veto held by the patricians over decisions by the assembly was removed and resolutions of the plebs were in certain circumstances turned into law for the whole people. There were measures in the later fourth century about interest rates and self-imposed debt slavery. Nevertheless, in 287 a major debt crisis precipitated the last of the three secessions, this time to the Janiculum hill on the far side of the Tiber. The crisis was remedied (we know not how), and, as a further concession, by a law of the dictator Hortensius the resolutions of the plebs were declared to be in future binding on the whole Roman people.

This was not the end to reforms to the republican constitution, but we may reasonably regard it now as fully formed. What was its nature? The assemblies, the democratic element, were fundamental but in many ways limited. They elected major and most minor magistrates; they passed laws that could change the constitution or even overthrow it; they were the venue for political trials, whether the penalty was capital or a fine. However, they did not have the dignity or scope for participation afforded to those in the Athenian democracy. Roman assemblies only met if summoned by a magistrate, whether this was to hear speeches or actually to take a decision. Those attending stood, not sat, and had no right to enter into the discussion. The agenda was the magistrate's which they could approve or reject. The only forum for free political discussion was the senate. This was no longer the preserve of patricians, nor did it retain any ultimate control over any political process. However, reforms to its membership may be seen to have increased its authority as a body comprising all those available with a distinguished military or political record or religious standing.

Although the senate was freer in debate than an assembly, it was still largely dependent on the consul or praetor who summoned it for its agenda and entirely dependent on the magistrates as a whole for the implementation of its decisions. In Polybius' view the consuls provided a monarchic element, in so far as they could exercise authority arbitrarily, something that might be detrimental if it was not at times frustrated by the senate and the assemblies. The Romans believed in strong executives, especially in the military field, and disliked divided decision making there (consuls did not normally act together in the same campaign). In principle, men were elected to do a job, rewarded with praise and further office if they succeeded, but punished if they failed.

It is an interesting feature of Roman culture, at least by the middle Republic, that even a great number of major religious functions, whether sacrifice or the consultation of divine approval through augury, was entrusted to magistrates and not priests. The importance of the individual is highlighted in stories dating from about the late fourth century found in the later Roman annals, where it is the charismatic individual who predominates, not the aristocracy or the people as a whole.

Already, at the end of the fourth century, we find in the consular lists plebeian families that continued to be significant into the late Republic, as were a number of the patricians. The plebeians joined the leading men in the senate. Was this then the substitution of one closed aristocracy for another? No: because ultimately the route to power and authority lay through popular election. The multiplication of great or formerly great families made the competition harder. The pursuit of a career in political and military command required a foundation of wealth. With these provisos, the way was open to talent. The Roman ideal for a man was *virtus*, a mixture of courage and skill in the military field with sound judgement and self-restraint in domestic politics and the family. Aristocrats claimed a *virtus* inherited from their ancestors, in particular the 'notables' or *nobiles* (for the most part the descendants of former consuls), but they had to prove and renew this by their own achievements. *Virtus* led to *fama* (good reputation) or *gloria*, which outlasted a man's mortal frame, whether it was preserved in an epitaph or the text of a funeral eulogy or, later, in the annals of Rome.

THREE

The Mastery of Italy

By 280 BC, a few years after Hortensius' legislation,
the year when King Pyrrhus of Epirus invaded Italy,
Rome had virtual dominion over the whole Italian
peninsula. This would have been hardly conceivable
in the fifth century. Then the foundation dates of
their early colonies show the Latins as a whole
securing their territory against the Aequi and Volsci
and in southern Latium. However, north-west of the
Tiber Rome herself was threatened by Veii, an
Etruscan city only 10 miles distant. She also had
difficulty in recovering from the Etruscans Fidenae
on the east bank of the Tiber. This was finally
achieved shortly before 400 BC and in about 390 the
Romans captured Veii itself. This was a landmark in
the growth of Roman power. The Romans destroyed
the city, after transferring a major cult (that of Juno
the Queen) to the Aventine hill at Rome. Its land
was added to Roman territory, providing immense

potential for agriculture and additional security against Etruscan attack. However, Rome had not had time to profit from her success when it was jeopardised by Gauls.

For some time before 400 Celtic peoples had been moving into Lombardy (hence the Romans called the area Cisalpine Gaul) and the northern Adriatic coast. However, the expedition of Brennus (387/6) seems to have been not a major migration but a journey by a warrior band, intending to take mercenary service with Dionysius the tyrant of Syracuse but enjoying any opportunity for enrichment it could. These Gauls attacked Clusium, defeated a Roman army at the River Allia 11 miles north of Rome (July 18) and entered the city, which did not have a complete circuit wall. Roman forces under M. Manlius held on to the Capitol, but the rest of the city was sacked. When they had acquired enough booty, the Gauls moved on, and the Romans who had evacuated the city returned under the leadership of M. Furius Camillus, the victor over Veii.

The Romans had to rebuild their city and make it more secure. This is probably the date of the construction of the so-called Servian Wall, made of tufa from the territory of Veii. This wall, remains of which can still be seen, would have been about 7 miles long and included most of the area then inhabited, although not the Campus Martius. Within a few years colonies had been placed to the north of Veientine land at Sutrium and Nepet.

Tusculum on the fringe of the Alban hills merged itself politically with Rome, Caere (Cerveteri) in southern Etruria became an ally, but the Romans found that their traditional enemies – Volsci, Aequi and Hernici – were now joined by rival Latin cities – Praeneste, Tibur and Velitrae. There were also further Gallic raids. After a series of victories Rome started to remodel the Latin League as an association no longer of theoretical equals but under Roman hegemony. By about 350 more distant cities in Etruria, Tarquinii and Falerii had come under Roman control, as did Sora and Privernum to the east and south of Latium. But a more striking development of foreign policy was their intervention in the rich area of Campania and their contact with the Samnites.

The Samnites were an Oscan-speaking people with fine fighting skills, who formed a federation of four tribes in the central Apennines. They lived in villages with an economy based on upland agriculture and stock raising. Religious centres, such as that at Pietrabbondante, must have also contributed to political unity. Rome apparently first became their ally in 348, perhaps because she wanted Samnite co-operation in coercing her discontented Latin allies and the hill peoples bordering Latium. Almost immediately (345) she broke this alliance in order to support the Campanians against them.

The interior of Campania had once been occupied by Etruscans, while the Greeks had settled on the coastline in cities such as Cumae and Neapolis (Naples). In the fifth century the area had been overrun by Oscan-speaking Sabellians, kin to the Samnites, but these had taken over much of the culture of the earlier settlers. Rome campaigned successfully on behalf of these Campanians, but then concluded a peace with the Samnites, which restored the former alliance (341). The Campanians, outraged by this double-dealing, formed an alliance with Rome's discontented Latin partners and revolted from Rome. The Romans won a decisive victory in Campania under P. Decius Mus in 340 and went on to reduce the Latin cities. In 338 the revolt was at an end and a new settlement was imposed on both Latium and Campania, which brought about a big accretion to Roman territory but is also interesting for the legal devices involved.

Some cities – Aricia, Lanuvium, Nomentum and Pedum – were simply absorbed into Roman territory and the Roman citizen body without qualification, becoming country towns in a state of which Rome was the capital. Others were incorporated in a more humiliating fashion, Antium losing its warships (their beaks became the *rostra* supporting the tribunal in the Forum Romanum) and Velitrae its aristocracy to the benefit of new Roman settlers. The remnants of the Latin League – Praeneste, Tibur and Latin colonies such as Cora, Norba and Ardea – remained Roman allies with theoretical independence but with *de facto* subjection in external affairs, and with the same special rights that previously Latin cities had shared. These were, first, the right of intermarriage (*conubium*), secondly, the right to own land in each other's territory and the right to use each other's legal procedures to enforce contracts, especially those that conveyed ownership of things such as land, slaves and horses (*commercium*), and thirdly, the right to migrate to another Latin community and take up citizenship there instead through formal registration.

A new status was devised for the Campanians and for the Volscian towns of Formiae and Fundi in the land between Latium and Campania. Their people became citizens without the vote, known also as *municipes* (those who undertake duties). They had the private rights of Roman citizens but no political rights, in that they neither voted in assemblies nor could undertake public office at Rome. Like Tusculum or Aricia, their towns retained a local administration that initially may not have changed much. However, their legal system was ultimately subject to Roman magistrates and they were probably pressed to make their procedures more Roman.

The Romans were thus equipped with consti-tutional mechanisms for absorbing or linking closely to Rome further territories in Italy. They might of course simply settle a body of citizens on new territory. These were 'Roman colonies', in this period usually small. Alternatively, they might either create a new 'Latin colony' from their own citizens or the Latin allies, or grant an existing community citizenship without the vote. Finally, there was the looser link of alliance. Apart from alliances made by equal contracting partners, a people might surrender itself to Rome, not after hostilities but in order to receive help, as the Campanians did in 345. This enabled the Romans to treat the others' territory as their own and fight for it without abandoning their theoretical principle of avoiding aggressive wars. Once secure, these allies had their territory and domestic independence restored to them and guaranteed by a treaty, which joined them permanently in a military pact with Rome. Defeated enemies, if their territory was not absorbed or colonised, were also granted a treaty, but one which openly stipulated subordination.

In the next sixty years, Rome built on these foundations her mastery of Italy. It was not simply a matter of military prowess. The mechanisms just outlined gave her a range of diplomatic strategies. However, every success brought increasing sources of manpower, which enabled her to outweigh opponents. She also developed an army whose strength lay in the tactical variety of its infantry. Each legion had three main ranks and a screen of skirmishers in front. The rear rank was equipped, like Greek heavily armed soldiers, with a large thrusting spear and shield; the two in front of it had a lighter spear that could be thrown as well as used hand to hand and made greater use of swords, probably imitating Rome's opponents in the Apennines.

Ten years later Roman relations with the Samnites had broken down over Samnite intervention in Rome's new territory and the creation of a Latin colony at Fregellae in formerly Samnite land. A long struggle ensued, in which Rome suffered one famous military humiliation at the Caudine Forks east of Campania in 321 but in the long run her attrition was successful, as was her complete subjection of her old enemies, the Aequi and Hernici. Central Apennines peoples, such as the Marsi and Paeligni were brought into alliance, there were the first conquests in northern Apulia and Lucania, and Rome's domains were secured by the creation of further colonies such as Terracina, Cales, Suessa Aurunca and Alba Fucens (the last deep in the Apennines).

In colonies of this time there is evidence for the earliest forms of the characteristic orthogonal Roman land division, still embedded now in the landscape. In this period too Roman roads were first established, for example the Via Appia to Campania (begun in 312) and the Via Valeria through the Apennines (307). Meanwhile, a major offensive by a group of Etruscan cities led to Roman victory (308) and all the Etruscans and some Umbrian cities were effectively made subject to Rome. In 298 Rome faced a further challenge: the Samnites took control in Apulia and Lucania and simultaneously encouraged an Etruscan revolt. The turning point in the war was a Roman victory over the Samnites and the Gauls who were supporting them at Sentinum in Umbria (295). A long process of conquest in Etruria, Sabine territory, Samnium itself, Apulia and Lucania was brought to an end by Manius Curius in 290.

In 284 Roman control in Etruria was jeopardised by a major Gallic invasion with Etruscan support. The Romans were defeated at Arretium (Arezzo), but the situation was recovered by victories that followed in the next two years, the first at Lake Vadimon, only 40 miles north of Rome. In 282, a campaign began with even more fateful consequences. Rome supported the oligarchic ruling group in the Greek city of Thurii against democrats backed by its Greek neighbour Tarentum (Taranto). This brought conflict with not only Tarentum, but a grand alliance of Samnites, Bruttians and Lucanians, eager to expel Roman influence from the south of Italy. Although Rome's armies were successful and she tried to negotiate a peace with Tarentum, the latter sought to preserve her freedom by calling in the aid of King Pyrrhus from Greece (281).

The war against Pyrrhus was to confirm Roman control of peninsular Italy. At the same time it brought Rome on to a larger stage as a Mediterranean power. Pyrrhus was not merely King of Epirus: he had been briefly King of Macedon itself in the 290s and was a significant player in the long power game that followed the death of Alexander the Great, the Wars of the Successors. His own forces were based on the Macedonian model, akin to those that under Alexander had carried western arms to Samarkand and the Indus. Pyrrhus was immediately victorious in 280 at Heraclea in southern Italy, but at considerable cost. He advanced as far as Praeneste in Latium, but could not get control of any cities there or in Campania. His offer of a negotiated peace, requiring Rome to cede her hegemony over the Samnites and Lucanians as well as restoring autonomy to the Greek cities, was rejected after the fabled intervention in the senate by Appius Claudius the Blind.

Pyrrhus' second victory at Ausculum in northern Apulia was even more costly to his manpower. Negotiations for peace once again failed, Rome preferring a new alliance with Carthage. Subsequent campaigning by C. Fabricius pinned Pyrrhus in southern Italy. In frustration Pyrrhus turned to aiding the Greek cities of Sicily against Carthage, but he was oppressive and unpopular with those he was supposed to be helping. Frustrated, he returned to Italy, where he was finally defeated by Manius Curius in 275 at Beneventum in southern Samnium.

After Pyrrhus' departure the next year most of the south Italians made peace with Rome and became her allies, although Tarentum held out until 272. Among the prisoners enslaved there was a boy who was subsequently educated at Rome and liberated from slavery. He became the first Roman to write poetry and plays on the Greek model in Latin, Livius Andronicus.

FOUR

The Era of the Punic Wars

The confirmation of Rome's power in Italy effected by the defeat of Pyrrhus led her almost immediately into wider conflicts that were to transform the balance of power in the Mediterranean. There was an element of chance in the conjunction of events, but conscious decisions, mainly made by the Romans themselves, were critical. Rome's new importance was signalled by her treaty in 273 with Ptolemy II Philadelphus, King of Egypt (Egypt was one of the three great powers in the Greek world at the time and important as an exporter of grain). Three years later the Romans recovered the Greek city of Rhegium (Reggio di Calabria) from its Campanian garrison. A few miles across the straits in Sicily another group of Campanians, former mercenaries of the Syracusan tyrant Agathocles, controlled Messana. They now came under attack by the new King of Syracuse, Hiero II, and sought help both from Carthage and from Rome (265).

Carthage lies on a promontory of land between the salt lake of Tunis and the sea. Its foundation by Phoenicians from Tyre was dated by ancient sources to the ninth century BC, though there is as yet no archaeological evidence for settlement earlier than the mid-eighth. The city was in a superb position for maritime communication and was backed by an agriculturally rich hinterland. The Carthaginians had dependencies in the Phoenician settlements in western Sicily, which they used as a basis for expansion and at times, especially in the fourth century, controlled most of the island. They also had settlements in Sardinia, Spain and the Balearic Islands.

When Messana was debated by the Romans, the citadel had already been handed over to a nearby Carthaginian force, but this goaded the Romans rather than deterring them. They had made a series of treaties with Carthage. The first two were largely concerned with regulating Roman trade with Punic possessions and Punic intervention in Italy, the last with a joint military effort against Pyrrhus. We are told that the Romans were frightened that Carthage would completely dominate Sicily, but the war was also advocated as a means to recover financial losses suffered in recent conflicts. The assembly voted to aid Messana and a Roman force crossed the straits (264). The Carthaginians withdrew but then put Messana under siege. So began the longest continuous war in the ancient world.

Most military activity was in the first fifteen years. A temporary alliance between Hiero and the Carthaginians collapsed after the Romans put Syracuse under siege and Hiero became a Roman ally instead (in 263). The new allies went on to capture Agrigentum from the Carthaginians after a long siege in which famine and disease weakened the armies on both sides. The victory, however, inspired the Romans to think of conquering the whole of Sicily and therefore in the winter of 262/1 they built a war fleet of their own for the first time (previously they had employed the ships of their Greek allies). They are said to have copied the pattern of a captured Punic ship, not implausibly, since we know that the Carthaginians assembled their ships from prefabricated parts. Roman crews were inexperienced both in rowing and naval warfare and the commanding magistrates often knew little of the sea. The initial Roman victory at Mylae in 260 was achieved by turning a sea battle

into a land battle through the use of spiked gang
planks (the commander C. Duilius commemorated
this with a column decorated with the 'beaks',
i.e. rams, of warships).

The Romans now made attacks on the Carthaginian
dependencies in Sardinia, while pressing northwards
and westwards into Punic Sicily by land. They also
made a more adventurous use of sea power, perhaps
hoping to end the war swiftly. A raid on Malta was
followed in 256 by a landing in Africa on the Cape
Bon peninsula led by M. Atilius Regulus. For a year
this comparatively small force held out, causing the
dismayed Carthaginians to take advice from a visiting
Spartan mercenary, but then the Romans were
tempted to do battle in the plain, where conditions
favoured the Punic cavalry and elephants: they were
defeated and Regulus captured. A Roman naval force
rescued the survivors but suffered heavy losses in a
storm on the way home.

In spite of their losses, there was another
unsuccessful Roman raid on Africa in 253 in the
region of the Punic cities near modern Tripoli. In
the meantime the Romans seized most of the
former Punic area of Sicily, including Panormus
(Palermo) and the Lipari islands. Only the major

Punic strongholds of Lilybaeum (Marsala) and Drepanum (Trapani) held out: the latter was the scene of a major Roman defeat at sea owing to an over-eager commander in 249, and in the same year another Roman fleet was driven on to a lee shore near Camarina and destroyed. The Romans maintained their sieges, harassed by the guerrilla tactics of Hamilcar Barca, but there was otherwise a lull in fighting while both Rome and Carthage built new fleets. At Rome this was by a 'private finance initiative', whose repayment depended on the outcome of the war. The war was ended by a Roman naval victory under C. Lutatius Catulus over a Carthaginian relief fleet at the Aegatian Isles west of Sicily in 242.

Under the terms of the treaty the Carthaginians were to refrain from attacking Syracuse, evacuate Sicily and the islands between Sicily and Italy, and pay an indemnity of 3,200 silver talents. However, there was worse to come. Financially exhausted, they were unable to pay off their mercenaries and these revolted, starting a bloodthirsty war that threatened the city of Carthage itself (the subject of Flaubert's novel *Salammbo*). Cities formerly allied to Carthage joined the rebels voluntarily or by compulsion; another group of mercenaries caused the secession of Sardinia.

The Carthaginians got support from Hiero of Syracuse, while Rome refused to intervene during the war, though invited to by the rebels (her traders were forced to desist from supplying the rebels). However, when Punic victory in Africa was assured after over three years fighting, the Romans changed policy and accepted from the mercenaries the surrender of Sardinia. Carthage objected, but Rome declared war, forcing a diplomatic climb-down and an additional indemnity of 1,200 talents. For the next eleven years (238–27) she was to campaign in both Sardinia and Corsica, eventually incorporating them into her empire as she had done the former Punic regions of Sicily. Meanwhile, in 237 Hamilcar Barca, the commander victorious over the mercenaries, was sent to govern the Punic possessions in Spain and took with him his nine-year-old son Hannibal.

Every major Roman victory had led to a change in the scale of her ambitions as well as of her strength. The First Punic War turned her into a leading maritime power, and not only in warships (Roman traders regularly visited Africa and are also attested in Greece). The expenses of the war were colossal: Rome lost 700 warships. Appropriately, it is in this period that we first have evidence for regular issues of silver and bronze coinage by Rome. Up to this time the main issuers of coinage in Italy had been the Greek cities. For almost half the Republic the Romans had relied on bronze bars, following the example of the Etruscans: they only issued silver in Campania in the late fourth century, then some silver and bronze at about the time of the Pyrrhic War. By the outbreak of the Second Punic War they had a coinage whose obverse type was a Roman deity, the reverse of the silver showing Jupiter in a four-horse chariot, the reverse of the bronze the prow of a warship. The coinage was primarily for military expenditure, but could also feed commerce. It is revealing that money lending at interest was now important enough to be regulated by a series of laws.

During the First Punic War Rome maintained her control of Italy, suppressing revolts at Volsinii in 265–4 and Falerii in 241. A number of colonies were founded in the third century, of two kinds: new cities with Latin rights such as Hadria (*c.* 283), Cosa and Paestum (273), Beneventum and Ariminum

(268), Brundisium (244) and Spoletium (241), and
small Roman colonies that were forts on the coast
such as Minturnae and Sinuessa (296), Sena Gallica
(*c.* 283), Alsium (247) and Fregenae (245).

Rome strengthened her position in relation to the
Gauls by first planting colonies on or near the
Adriatic coast and then settling the so-called 'Gallic
land' south of Ariminum with Roman citizens. This
was the project of C. Flaminius (tribune in 232),
who was simultaneously cultivating popular support
for himself by satisfying land-hunger. The last
independent Gallic invasion was defeated at
Telamon in Etruria in 225 and Roman commanders,
including Flaminius (consul in 223), carried the war
into Liguria and the Po valley. As censor in 220,
Flaminius built a new road up the Tiber into Umbria
and then across to the Adriatic and Ariminum.

At the beginning of the Second Punic War (218)
the Romans had just founded Latin colonies at
Cremona and Placentia (Piacenza) and were
dividing land at Mutina (Modena), thus establishing
a foothold in Cisalpine Gaul. They had also for the
first time created a protectorate east of the Adriatic,
in response to the harassment of their traders by
the Illyrians and appeals for help from Greek cities

and other peoples in the area. An expedition made in 229/8 against the Illyrian Queen Teuta led to the Romans establishing Demetrios of Pharos as the chief authority in the region in her place. However, he changed his loyalties in favour of Macedon and in 219 the Romans expelled him from Pharos in the interest of their Greek friends.

Rome, however, had more serious concerns west of Italy. Apart from her recent seizure of Sardinia and Corsica, she had a longstanding connection with Massilia (Marseilles), a Greek city with a string of associated trading stations along the south coast of France and the Costa Brava. She was clearly disturbed by the successful Punic expansion in Spain under Hamilcar Barca and, later, his son-in-law Hasdroubal to the extent that at the time of the great Gallic invasion of 225 she made an agreement with Hasdroubal that he should not cross the Ebro northwards under arms. At about this time she also took under her protection Saguntum, a city on the coast to the south of the Ebro. In 221 Hasdroubal was murdered by a disgruntled Celt and Hannibal took over command of the army.

Hannibal himself claimed that he had been brought up by his father to be an implacable enemy of Rome. Pro-Roman sources assume that he was already planning a revanchist war to put right the injustices Carthage had suffered. However, it is equally made clear that the Romans believed a new war inevitable and were prepared to undertake this in Spain, using Saguntum as a base, had not Hannibal anticipated them by attacking Saguntum himself. Warned by the Saguntines, Rome had sent an embassy to Hannibal at New Carthage (Cartagena) in the winter of 220/19 demanding that he should leave the city alone and forbidding him to cross the Ebro. These demands were repeated at Carthage itself on the embassy's journey home. However, once it had gone, Hannibal besieged Saguntum and captured it in eight months.

Rome did not try to help the city directly, but instead made preparations and at the beginning of 218 sent a second embassy with an ultimatum to the Carthaginian senate, requiring the surrender of Hannibal and his advisers as treaty breakers if war was to be avoided. The Carthaginians stood firm, maintaining that the dispute fell outside any agreement that had been properly ratified at Carthage. So began a war, which became the most complex in antiquity and probably the most costly.

It was not a war in which either side sought to destroy the other utterly. The Carthaginians hoped to break up Rome's power base in Italy and so recover their own lost possessions; the Romans wished to preserve what they had and to reduce or eliminate Carthage's military potential. Moreover, they soon realised the importance of the resources of Spain, which they wanted for themselves.

Initially, however, Hannibal's dramatic march on Italy over the Pyrenees and Alps appeared to threaten Rome's very survival. The Romans hoped to campaign aggressively in Spain and Africa; the news of Hannibal's march led instead to an unsuccessful attempt to cut him off at the Rhône. When this failed, most Roman troops were concentrated in northern Italy. Hannibal arrived with some 20,000 infantry and 6,000 cavalry surviving of his own, but was reinforced by Gauls with whom he had been negotiating. Before the end of 218 he had won two victories in the Po valley, a cavalry engagement at the River Ticinus and a major battle at the Trebia. His infantry was inferior to the Romans but he had superb Numidian cavalry, good light-armed troops and above all his own ingeniousness and flexibility as a commander.

The Romans did detach forces for service in Spain under two brothers, Publius and Cnaeus Scipio, but Hannibal was their chief focus. The following year he crossed the Apennines and entrapped the consular army of C. Flaminius between the mountains and Lake Trasimene. This great victory allowed him to move south, though he avoided Rome and Roman allies were still loyal. Quintus Fabius Maximus was appointed dictator and adopted his famous strategy of delay, stalking Hannibal but refusing battle. In 216 Rome returned to an aggressive approach against Hannibal who by then was in Apulia. The two consuls Varro and Aemilius Paulus, with some 80,000 men, were defeated on the plain of Cannae by an encircling movement and Roman losses were immense (2 August 216). This led to the secession of most of Rome's allies in southern Italy, including the Campanians who had Roman citizenship without the vote, but not the Latin colonies.

This is the point when, in Polybius' view, Rome was saved by her constitution. She was so short of manpower that criminals and debtors were released from prison and boys were recruited as if they had reached manhood. She was also short of money.

Within a few years the bronze coinage (the *as*) became fiduciary, being devalued to half its former weight, and a new silver coinage of full value (the *denarius*) was introduced and declared equivalent to ten *asses*. The holding of precious metal and jewellery by individuals was limited. Rich men were required to supply their slaves for naval service and pay them. Military contractors were required to supply arms and clothing on credit.

For the next few years Rome was reduced to minimising her losses as her power in various regions came under threat. In Italy she could not for several years recover Capua and Campania, there was a further serious defeat in south Italy and the port of Tarentum was lost. In Sicily, Hiero of Syracuse, who had been supplying Rome with great quantities of grain, died; after various intrigues his successor Hieronymus was murdered, and Syracuse defected to Carthage. However, Hannibal also had one major problem, a lack of adequate reinforcement in Italy. Cavalry, elephants, money and grain arrived from Carthage in 215, but later expeditions were diverted to Spain, Sardinia and Sicily. Hasdroubal was prevented by the Scipios from leaving Spain immediately to join Hannibal in Italy. Philip V of

Macedon made a military alliance with Hannibal, but this proved delusive. In spite of success in Illyria, Philip could not cross the Adriatic.

The critical year was 211. Syracuse fell to Rome after a long siege owing to an outbreak of plague, and Punic gains in Sicily were subsequently recovered. Capua also fell, in spite of Hannibal's diversionary tactic of a sudden march on Rome. In Greece Rome made an alliance with the Aetolians and began to orchestrate a campaign that was to tie Philip down defending his own sphere of power. There had been disaster for the Romans in southern Spain, where both Scipios were defeated and killed in 212 but the Romans sent out Publius' son, another P. Cornelius Scipio, later called Africanus, as a replacement and he quickly took the fight to the Carthaginians. In 209 he captured New Carthage; the next year he won a victory at Baecula in Andalucia, after which Hasdroubal Barca at last chose to leave Spain to join Hannibal in Italy. In 206 Scipio completed the subjection of Punic Spain and was able to return to Rome.

Meanwhile, in Italy fortunes had oscillated: the Romans had recovered Tarentum but had lost two of their commanders in a battle and an ambush.

Hannibal's influence was limited but Rome and Italy were exhausted. When Hasdroubal arrived in northern Italy in 207, his way was blocked south of Ariminum. At this point the consul who had been shadowing Hannibal in the south managed to remove a portion of his forces and lead them north to join his colleague. The combined Roman armies then defeated Hasdroubal at the River Metaurus (23 June 207).

Although Hannibal remained unsubdued, Punic pressure on Italy was now eased. The war in Greece was also brought to an end by a peace agreement. When Scipio returned from Spain to be elected consul in 205, his military command was originally to be in southern Italy facing Hannibal, but on request he was granted permission to invade Africa, though only with volunteer troops. While in Spain he had made contact with the Numidian princes Syphax and Massinissa, who controlled the hinterland of Carthaginian territory and, moreover, supplied the crack Punic cavalry. Syphax was brought back to his Punic allegiance, but Massinissa came to assist Scipio when he landed in Africa near Utica in 204. Scipio at first had little success but the following year, after destroying the opposition camps, he secured a victory over the Carthaginians and Syphax inland in the Medjerda valley and later helped Massinissa to seize the kingship of Numidia. An attempt to make a negotiated peace failed: it was ratified at Rome but rejected by the Carthaginian people, who summoned back Hannibal from Italy.

In 202 Hannibal landed his veterans from Italy near Hadrumetum (Sousse). He received Punic and Numidian reinforcements and with these he confronted Scipio at Zama in central Tunisia. The Numidian cavalry on either side neutralised each other; Hannibal's elephants were rendered innocuous; ultimately it became a soldiers' battle, in which the Roman infantry was superior. The peace terms were a more severe version of those on offer the previous year. Carthage was to lose her empire, her sovereignty being confined to the area within the 'Punic trenches' in northern and eastern Tunisia, and to have no independent foreign policy, even in Africa; she was also to lose her war fleet, except a symbolic ten ships, and to pay an indemnity of 10,000 silver talents over a period of fifty years.

This is rightly considered one of the decisive wars in world history. In Polybius' view, the victors now thought that the world lay at their feet. Their success can be ascribed to their massive supplies of manpower, their superiority at sea, but above all to their coherence as a society. The machinery of their government continued to work and permitted a number of innovations in military command. The people were largely in agreement in making personal sacrifices. Aristocratic rivalries did not cease, but the senate gained immensely in standing as a forum for policy and the reconciliation of differences, while the plebs retained their fundamental political rights. Finally, the resistance to Hannibal owed much to the stubborn obstinacy that characterised Roman behaviour.

FIVE

The Dominion of the Mediterranean

Within less than two years from the settlement with Carthage Rome was again involved in a major war – with Philip V of Macedon. Since the time of the war with Pyrrhus she had had contacts as a state with the eastern Mediterranean, while individual Romans and Italians are also attested there, mainly as traders. However, it was a striking re-orientation of her politics that for the next fifty years Rome was to be more concerned with this world than with the western Mediterranean that had recently fallen under her sway.

The opening was provided by relations between the main near-eastern powers and their effect on the friends Rome had previously acquired. The new King of Egypt, Ptolemy V Epiphanes, was a minor. In 203–2, shortly after his accession, Philip V had made an alliance with Antiochus III (the Great) of Syria, whose effect was that they would not impede each other in expansion in the Aegean and Asia Minor. Antiochus was mainly concerned with Asia Minor, where there were the dependent cities of Egypt and Rhodes, Philip with the Aegean, where he most directly affected Rhodian interests. The plans of both kings threatened Attalus I, the King of Pergamum in north-west Asia Minor. Egypt's alliance with Rome had been cemented by the provision of grain during the Second Punic War; Attalus had become a Roman ally in the fighting against Macedon; Rhodes had a long-standing friendship with Rome. It was further claimed that Macedonian volunteers had fought with Hannibal at Zama and that Philip had been tampering with the independence of Greek cities on the Adriatic coast, which had been guaranteed by the peace in 206–5.

A Roman embassy had reached Greece at the end of winter in 200 when Athens was attacked by one of Philip's commanders in consequence of a quarrel over an alleged violation of the Eleusinian mysteries. The embassy went on to meet Philip at Abydos and declared war on him, after he refused to accept an ultimatum that would have required him to stop making war on Greeks and reach a settlement with Attalus. Meanwhile, at Rome the military assembly had been persuaded with difficulty at the second attempt to vote for a new war against Philip. Beneath the tissue of pretexts can be detected Rome's desire to repay Philip for his support for Hannibal and the confidence in her power that the victory over Carthage had created. The plebs may have been war weary, but the older and wealthier Romans, who were preponderant in that assembly and for the most part would not have to do the fighting, saw a new opportunity.

The beginning of the war was an anti-climax for the Romans. In spite of some minor successes they found it difficult to fight their way into Macedonia through the mountains from the West. However, after refusing to join the Romans the Aetolians began a war with Philip of their own. In 198 Titus Quinctius Flamininus confronted Philip at the Aous gorge and in negotiations put forward tougher terms than before the war, requiring Philip to relinquish his control of Thessaly. Rome's navy and her allies prepared to attack Philip's stronghold at Corinth and this brought the Achaean League – the

group of cities who united much of the Peloponnese
– to the Roman side. Later in the year Flamininus
and Philip faced each other in Thessaly. Philip
sought a negotiated peace over the winter but was
met with ever-increasing Roman demands tending to
the liberation of Greece from Macedon. In 197
Flamininus defeated Philip in the field at
Kynoskephalai in Thessaly (the elaborate and
formidable Macedonian military machine was
worsted by the more flexible Roman force on
uneven ground). Rome was now free to impose a
settlement in Greece. It went even further than the
Greeks expected.

Philip was required to become a Roman ally,
paying an indemnity of 1,000 talents, surrendering
his fleet, evacuating his fortresses in Greece and
Greek cities both in Greece and Asia Minor. This
liberation of Greece was proclaimed by Flamininus
at the Isthmus in spring 196. Rome appeared to
have decisively reversed the result of Philip II's
victory over the Greeks in 338. However, the liberty
offered was in fact similar to that granted to Greek
cities from time to time in the intervening period by
the dynasties who succeeded to Alexander the
Great's empire. Cities were to have their own laws

and local politics, to be free from garrisons and Roman taxes. They were, however, implicitly the military allies of Rome without any formal treaty. Moreover, it soon became apparent that, given the opportunity, Rome would encourage the creation of local constitutions that she approved (which tended towards oligarchy rather than democracy) and support politicians whom she herself trusted. In particular, she attacked and weakened her former ally, the Spartan tyrant Nabis, who had at first joined Philip in the war. Her objectives achieved, Rome withdrew her legions in 194. Meanwhile, in Greece Flamininus' head had appeared on coins, a victory ode had been written to him and games had been established in his honour as a quasi-divine personage.

Unsolved problems, however, soon required the legions' return. The Aetolians had lent Rome military aid in the hope of taking over some of Philip's cities in the ensuing settlement, but the policy of freedom for the Greeks denied them this. Furthermore, the Romans were drawn by their policies into a worsening diplomatic clash with Antiochus the Great of Syria. In 197 he had taken over coastal cities in Asia Minor south and north of

Pergamum and then moved on into the Chersonese (Gallipoli peninsula) and the coast of Thrace, taking over European cities that had most recently been Philip's. His success disturbed both Rhodes and the new King of Pergamum, Eumenes II. Philip's defeat had left a power vacuum into which Antiochus might be further tempted to expand.

Rome now exploited the 'freedom of the Greeks' as a diplomatic lever, arguing in a series of negotiations that Greek cities everywhere, including Asia Minor, should be autonomous, and in particular that Antiochus had no right to Philip's cities in Europe and no business in Europe at all. This was popular among Greeks, but not with Antiochus, who argued that he was merely resuming control of his ancestors' former dependencies. Suspicion was created when Hannibal, forced out of Carthage by political opponents, arrived at Antiochus' court in 195. Finally, in 192 the Aetolians tried to create a revolt against the Roman settlement and then requested Antiochus to send an army to liberate Greece.

Antiochus had had little success in acquiring adherents (Philip in particular had no love for him and remained loyal to Rome), when a Roman army

arrived under Acilius Glabrio in 191. It had no
difficulty in defeating the comparatively small
Syrian army at Thermopylai. The following year a
Roman army and fleet, strongly reinforced by
Pergamum and Rhodes, carried the war into Asia. It
was led by the brother of the victor over Hannibal,
Lucius Cornelius Scipio, who had Africanus himself
as one of his chief officers. The Roman alliance won
naval victories (perhaps the occasion of the
dedication of the famous 'Victory of Samothrace'
now in the Louvre) and a major victory on land at
Magnesia by Mount Sipylus.

The peace terms now imposed were simple but
drastic. Antiochus had to pay an indemnity – 15,000
talents to Rome and an amount of grain to
Eumenes – and to evacuate Asia Minor north and
west of the Taurus mountains. This was to the profit
of Pergamum and Rhodes, since cities that had not
voluntarily joined the Roman cause were divided
between them. Syrian power now only affected the
extreme east of the Mediterranean. Scipio's
successor, Cn. Manlius Vulso, while overseeing the
implementation of the treaty, marched into central
Anatolia to defeat the Celtic Galatians who were a
potential threat to Pergamum. Meanwhile, the

Aetolians after fruitless attempts to negotiate were gradually reduced until the fall of Ambracia in 189 brought about their final surrender.

Roman relations with Macedon and the Greek cities now entered a confused period in which there was no challenge to Rome's ultimate power in the area, should she have chosen to use it, but there were no magistrates exercising direct control, only visiting embassies. The Achaean League in particular explored the limits of its freedom, seeking to establish a friendly regime in Sparta (brought into the League during the war with Aetolia and Syria) in face of hostility from the friends of the former tyrants, and also to maintain its control of Messenia. Undermined by Roman diplomacy and local resistance, it failed and its distinguished leader Philopoemen was killed. Finally, in 180 a pro-Roman Achaean politician, Callistratus, when on an embassy to Rome, urged the senate to make plain what policies it wanted the Greek states to pursue.

Meanwhile, Rome's relations with Macedon began to deteriorate. Philip had seized towns outside the borders of Macedon as prizes during the war with Antiochus, especially in Thrace, but was subsequently forced to evacuate these in 184–3. His son Demetrius, who was cultivating and being cultivated by the Romans, was killed on Philip's orders in 180 for his disloyalty to Macedon. After Philip's death in 179, his other son Perseus improved Macedon's army and control of its borders and was diplomatically active in the Greek world, providing an alternative focus for those discontented with Rome. He intervened in civil strife in Thessaly, assisted Aetolia, allied with Boeotia and almost achieved an alliance with the Achaean League.

Roman suspicions were inflamed by Eumenes of Pergamum, who claimed that Perseus had attempted to get him assassinated. Rome duplicitously bought time by diplomacy in order to prepare war with Perseus in 172 but by the end of the year the Third Macedonian War had begun. Rome's successes in the field were at first limited. Illyria and much of Epirus joined the Macedonian side. However, in 169 the consul Q. Marcius Philippus found a way through the Olympus range into lower Macedonia and the following year L. Aemilius Paulus was victorious over Perseus at Pydna. The Illyrians were also defeated. In the same year Rome used the threat of war to stop an invasion of Egypt by the Syrian King Antiochus IV.

Macedonia was divided into four separate republics, paying to Rome half the taxes formerly paid to Perseus; Illyria too was divided into three. During the war the Romans had made it clear that they were marking down friends and enemies in the Greek world. Now came reprisals. As many as 1,000 dissident citizens of the Achaean League were deported to Italy, including the historian Polybius. In Epirus 70 towns were given over to plunder and 150,000 Epirots enslaved. At Rhodes, which had tried to mediate during the war, the politicians responsible were condemned to death under Roman pressure. The Romans also stripped Rhodes of dependent towns on the mainland and in 164 set up the island of Delos as a free port, thus taking away much of Rhodes' commercial supremacy. Rome was no longer for the Greeks the liberator even in appearance, but a ruthless imperial power of the traditional kind.

In the West, meanwhile, there had been no room for illusion. The Gallic alliance with Hannibal spurred the Romans on to establish their power even more firmly in Liguria, Venetia and the

Po Valley. There were new colonies such as Bononia (Bologna) and, at the head of the Adriatic, Aquileia. Moreover, a large number of Roman citizens were settled on plots of land near the new Via Aemilia (187) which led from Ariminum north-west through Cisalpine Gaul to Bononia and Placentia. On the west coast the Via Aurelia was extended north to Genua and from there the Via Postumia (148) linked Genua to Cremona. Spain was divided into two military commands ('provinces') in 197. Regular campaigning carried Roman arms deep into the interior of the peninsula from the eastern and southern coasts; taxation gradually became more systematic and Spain's mineral resources were exploited.

Here, as well as in Sicily, Sardinia and Corsica, there was direct subjection of conquered territory to Roman magistrates. This did not entail an elaborate system of administration. Even exact boundaries were unclear in continental areas. The governor, assisted by a deputy, his quaestor, maintained obedience to Rome, dispensed justice where he thought proper or was asked to intervene, and supervised the collection of revenue, whether this was direct – based on property or produce – or indirect – in the form of tolls or harbour dues. Forms of taxation varied from province to province (in Sicily it was based on that of the Syracusan tyrants). Rome relied on the existence of cities or other communities to provide a medium through which she could articulate her power.

So far in Africa and the Greek world there were no regular Roman magistrates. This changed in the middle of the century. Carthage had prospered in spite of paying a vast indemnity to Rome. Intermittent friction had arisen with Rome's favoured ally, King Masinissa of Numidia, over claims to territory. This flared up again in 153. Dissatisfied with earlier unfair Roman arbitrations, Carthage broke her treaty with Rome by using force against Masinissa. This provided a heaven-sent pretext for Romans like Cato the Censor, who were worried by Carthage's revival, and in 149 an expedition was sent to Africa. The city of Utica went over to Rome and Carthage herself at first surrendered, but faced with the Roman demand to move the city 10 miles from the sea – a warrant for its economic destruction – put itself into a state of siege. This proved frustrating for the Romans until they entrusted command to another Scipio –

Aemilianus, the adoptive grandson of Africanus –
who finally stormed Carthage and took it after a
week of house-to-house fighting in the spring of
146. The city was then razed to the ground and
Punic territory became another province.

In the same year the same fate befell Corinth,
and the freedom of Greece was no longer even an
illusion. In 149 a certain Andriscus had claimed the
throne of Macedon, defeating a Roman army, but
the next year had been himself defeated and killed.
Further south, after a dispute between the Achaean
League and Sparta, which wanted to secede, had
been referred to Rome, a Roman embassy finally
came to the League in 147, instructing that not only
Sparta, but Corinth, Argos and other cities should
be detached from it. These instructions were
rejected amid violent threats to the ambassadors.
The following year Rome declared war. The
Achaeans with great popular enthusiasm resisted
but were duly crushed by a new army sent from
Rome. In consequence Macedonia became a
province and its governor also took responsibility
for Greece. Some Greek territory was annexed by
Rome; the leagues were dissolved, and, while
certain cities and regions retained their former

status, in others new oligarchic governments were installed.

The year of the destruction of Carthage was taken by ancient historians as a turning point in the history of the Republic. In their view, up to that point the existence of serious rivals had demanded moral and political discipline at Rome. The elimination of external threats, however, not only betokened a new brutal form of imperial rule but left the way open for ruthless exploitation of the empire and for ambition, greed, luxury and consequential civil strife to flourish at Rome. What had been the nature of Roman society thus far?

In the third century the political conflicts characteristic of the Conflict of the Orders had become rare. Many of the material wants of the plebs were being satisfied by the profits of conquest. The leading plebeians had formed with the patricians a new governing class, whose success bred solidarity. Political success was associated with the holding of magistracies and winning of victories, duly recorded on monuments, statues, pictures and tombs. Politicians operated as individuals, but the aristocracy as a whole built up traditions, embodied above all in the business of the senate and the priesthoods. There were inevitably groupings of aristocrats, but their significance is far from clear. Friendships were made and broken, great men had lesser men as acolytes, and these connections might be repeated in later generations. They were particularly visible in the pursuit of magistracies, where families might co-ordinate their electoral muscle. We do not know how significant the votes that could be mustered from clients were. What can be seen is the rise of allegedly improper electoral methods from about 200 onwards, where candidates used their wealth in distributions, dinners and the holding of games in order to transcend any pre-existing relations of dependence. This created mobility among clients.

The aristocracy was gradually penetrated from below by 'new men', of whom Cato the Censor was the outstanding example. Born in Tusculum, he rose through the magistracies to the consulship (195) and the censorship (184), using his oratorical ability to conduct political feuds; a historian, he also wrote the first Roman work on agriculture. There was nothing resembling a modern political party, nor was it even certain that those who stood for office together were in agreement on policies, since elections were about personalities. Although most decisions about foreign policy took place in the Senate, the popular assemblies were responsible for a wide range of statutes concerning citizenship, colonies, land and the law itself. These were mostly put forward by tribunes and on a number of occasions were controversial. Tribunes might also show their teeth by protecting those who resisted conscription.

Meanwhile, Roman and Italian society and culture were changing. The conservatism of Roman religion was tempered by the public adoption of certain foreign cults, notably the cult of the Great Mother (*Magna Mater*) from central Asia Minor. By contrast the cult of Dionysus as Bacchus, which involved nightly meetings, including both men and women, and was popular among the plebs, was severely controlled. Empire was funding a more luxurious lifestyle among the aristocracy, but this was still in its infancy. Mosaic pavements and columns of African marble only seem to have become a fashion after 146. House prices at Rome were low. The public buildings of the city were still mostly small and unspectacular (the aqueducts were perhaps the chief exception). However, it was from the early second century that the Romans developed the use of concrete (mortared rubble) as a rapid and flexible form of construction that was in due course to transform Rome.

Greek intellectual culture was now making a significant impact. Since Livius Andronicus epic, tragedy and Greek-style comedy were written in Latin. The first histories of Rome, written in Greek in about 200, were now joined by Latin works, notably the 'Origins' of Cato. Aristocrats numbered Greek philosophers, such as the Stoic Panaetius, among their friends and the influence of philosophy may be detected in other intellectual fields. Interest in definition and forms of reasoning can be found in the development of the civil law by the earliest Roman jurists. These techniques, in conjunction with those more particular to public speaking, also formed part of the science of rhetoric that was taking root at Rome by the end of the second century. Not least, the stories of Rome's origins had been made to fit into Greek mythology, so that the Latin race could be said to be founded by the Trojan Aeneas near the end of the Bronze Age, 400 years before the foundation of Rome by Romulus.

SIX

From the Gracchi to Marius

It is debatable whether imperial success perverted Roman morality or merely gave new scope for existing failings; it is certain that it overthrew traditional society in Rome and Italy. The bulk of Rome's manpower had been peasant farmers working small plots of land in Roman territory or that of her colonies. Roman infantrymen were required to perform six years of military service, not necessarily in one sequence. When campaigns had been near home, this had not been too disruptive, as the year was in effect the summer months. Overseas campaigning and the demands of facing Hannibal had changed this. After the Punic Wars, although service beyond the norm was only rarely demanded in a crisis, fighting in remote parts of the Mediterranean was inevitably disruptive to the peasant's life, meaning that he could neither farm nor raise children in that period. Moreover, peasant land holdings were threatened by the rich, who sought legally or illegally to absorb them. They wished to find a safe investment for the money that flowed in from abroad: land was a traditional repository of wealth and brought more lustre to its owner than money out on loan or chests of silver.

The landowners pursued a more rational approach to farming, attested in Cato's handbook on agriculture, mixing forms of agriculture and stock raising on their estates and producing for the market rather than family consumption. Slaves, as well as free tenants, had probably formed part of the labour force of the rich before, but now they were preferred because they were available and cheap in the wake of conquest (this had its dangers: a massive slave revolt in Sicily and south Italy in 137 lasted about five years). For these reasons many small farmers were driven off the land. However, we should not exaggerate: archaeology shows that many others survived in various regions in Italy. Their decline was perhaps most pronounced close to Rome and also in those parts of Italy where there was specialisation in stock raising – a profitable enterprise undertaken chiefly for making leather and wool and thus contributing to production for the army. Slaves had been a feature of Roman society before, as of other Mediterranean societies, but their importance for these forms of production, and for the crafts and professions that multiplied in Rome, transformed the Roman economy and demography, not least because their frequent manumission at a price (economically rational, when the supply was so good) filled the citizen body with men of slave descent. Rome was in any case a magnet. Its wealth encouraged the growth of luxury trades, while construction and transport (especially through the docks) required free labour. The former slaves whom their owners liberated contributed also to the expansion of population, although the unhealthy living conditions must have taken a steady toll.

There was a special problem over Roman public land. This product of conquest had not always been assigned or sold but had been left as common land for anyone to exploit either through agriculture or grazing animals, limits being placed on each. Rich men with labour available had seized this in illegal quantities. A land bill was proposed in 140 but withdrawn. Then in 133 Tiberius Sempronius Gracchus, a plebeian noble from the heart of the aristocracy, proposed as tribune that the former limits on holdings of public land and the grazing of animals there should be enforced (some relaxation was permitted to those with children); the land so recovered was to be distributed in allotments to the landless. Opposed by rich landowners, he avoided discussion in the senate, but legislated directly through the plebeian assembly – a measure not illegal but provocative to his opponents (popular politics had been evident a few years earlier in resistance to conscription for the war in Spain and the passing of two bills about secret ballot).

Tiberius passed the bill after getting the assembly to depose another tribune who had been encouraged to veto it. When obstructed in its implementation, he proposed to exploit the revenues of the kingdom of Pergamum, which had been recently left to Rome on the death of its last king. He finally stood for an abnormal second tribunate with radical new proposals, bitter opposition led to violence and on the day of the election he was murdered by a mob of senators and their henchmen led by the chief pontiff Scipio

Nasica. There was subsequently a witch-hunt of his supporters by a special tribunal under the consuls of 132.

Tiberius was seen by his opponents as a tyrant, because he was a demagogue who sought to dominate politics, like certain notorious figures in Greek and early Roman history. Demagogues were often associated with the redistribution of land, and Tiberius had breached other political norms in deposing a colleague and seeking re-election. Nevertheless, his bill was put into effect and much land was redistributed, the main problem being opposition from dispossessed Italians.

Relations between Rome and her allies added a further dimension to the problems of rural Italy. Since the Second Punic War Rome had intervened more and more in the internal affairs of her Latin and Italian allies, often, but not always, at their request. Their citizens formed two-thirds of Rome's armies. Italians, although they had no automatic rights to booty, had profited from the expansion of the empire: their towns and shrines are evidence of this. They also began to assimilate the Latin language and Roman traditions. Nevertheless, they lacked the status that Roman citizenship conferred.

They did not have the political rights of voting or standing for Roman office. They had no protection from arbitrary action by Roman magistrates, no right to intermarry with Romans, no right to be owners, as opposed to tenants, of Roman land (the last two rights were possessed by Latins).

The issue was first crystallized in 125 when the consul M. Fulvius Flaccus proposed that allied communities should choose between being awarded Roman citizenship or *provocatio* (protection against Roman magistrates). The first would entail absorption and the loss of local independence, the second a limited increase in status. In the event the bill seems never to have been put to the vote, and a law was passed by Iunius Pennus expelling non-Romans from residence in Roman towns. In the same year an apparently prosperous Latin colony, Fregellae, seceded amid discontent among other Latin communities. This was futile, and Fregellae in the end was razed to the ground like Carthage and Corinth.

The younger brother of Tiberius Gracchus, Gaius, was quaestor in that year and opposed Pennus' law; then, after serving in Sardinia, he was elected tribune for 123 and re-elected in that year for 122. His two magistracies produced the largest and most significant amount of legislation sponsored by any politician during the Republic. Some measures sprang from his brother's policies and the reaction to them. He strengthened the *provocatio* laws, forbidding the capital condemnation of Roman citizens without popular approval and providing for the prosecution of offending magistrates. A new agrarian law, involving colonial settlements, was introduced and supported by a law promoting the building of roads. Among other measures the most significant were those about grain, the province of Asia, the province of Africa, the courts and the proposal about the Latins and allies.

The city now needed to import grain from abroad to survive. The price of this would tend to vary in proportion to the time elapsed since the last harvest. Gaius provided for the building of granaries and the sale of grain from these to Romans at a moderately subsidised price throughout the year. Rome had proceeded with the annexation of Pergamum, as the province of Asia, in the face of a prolonged nationalist revolt originally led by Aristonicus, a bastard son of

Eumenes II. When a final settlement for the province was discussed, Gaius proposed that the contracts for the collection of both direct and indirect taxes should be auctioned at Rome among syndicates of wealthy Romans. The contractors themselves came from the order of 'knights', i.e. the wealthiest Romans who were not senators. This order benefited also from Gaius' innovation in criminal justice. Traditionally, trials for political crimes had been held before assemblies, but in the second century many of them came to be handled by special tribunals with juries of varying sizes: in particular the recovery of money from Romans who had improperly exacted it from allies (*pecuniae repetundae*) had been the task of a permanent jury court since 149. Gaius revolutionised procedure in this court, permitting allies themselves to prosecute and offering them rewards for success (apart from the, now penal, damages), introducing a large jury of fifty and staffing this from a panel of 'knights', none of whom had any close connection with a senator. The likelihood of a senator being condemned for misconduct was greatly increased.

In Africa Gaius sought to found on the site of Carthage the first overseas Roman colony and settle

many Romans on the land there. The revival of
Carthage on a site that had been cursed caused
disquiet and led to sinister rumours in 122. In this
year Gaius, with the support of Fulvius Flaccus as
another tribune, tried to pass a more modest bill
about the Latins and Italians: only the Latins,
Rome's kith and kin, were to have full citizenship,
the Italians were to have some sort of voting rights.
This ran into formidable opposition (led by a
tribune, Livius Drusus) and did not succeed. In 121,
when Gaius was out of office, a tribune proposed
the repeal of his African law and violence broke out
between his and Gaius' supporters. The consul
Opimius obtained an emergency decree from the
senate, urging him to defend the Republic, and
used this to justify making war on Gaius' supporters
in Rome. Fulvius Flaccus was among those killed in
the fighting, Gaius committed suicide and
numerous of his supporters were executed on the
orders of the consul after investigation by a
tribunal. The African bill was repealed, but only in
relation to the re-founding of Carthage: the new
settlers were allowed to enjoy their landholdings.

After the death of Gaius much of his legislation
remained in place. The grain bill seems to have

been eventually rescinded, but revived in 100. The redistribution of land was in due course brought to an end. However, the Asian arrangements survived, while the new form of the recovery court continued and was a model for other courts handling different crimes, although senators were later to return as jurors. Nevertheless, Gaius' elimination constituted a reassertion of the collective authority of the aristocracy against the exploitation of the popular assembly by men who were themselves of the elite. These so-called 'populars' never constituted a party or even a continuous political inheritance, but an ideology of using the assemblies to legislate for the benefit of the people was now established. As for the aristocracy, its traditional domination of politics was again to be undermined, this time by military failure in Africa and on Rome's northern frontier.

After Masinissa's death in 149 the kingdom of Numidia had passed to Micipsa and then (117) was shared among Micipsa's two sons and bastard nephew Jugurtha, the last being not only a more capable and forceful personality but one who had useful connections with Romans through military service. Jugurtha eliminated one rival with Roman acquiescence; in removing the second he killed a number of Italian businessmen at the same time. Rome declared war in 111 but, when Jugurtha hastily surrendered, he was at first restored to the kingdom. There was an outcry at Rome about his corruption of leading senators and a special tribunal was set up by plebiscite to investigate this, which condemned Opimius among others; as for Jugurtha, after an attempt to extract evidence from him failed, the war was renewed.

Jugurtha was too mobile for the somewhat pedestrian Roman forces. Progress was finally made in tracking Jugurtha by Q. Metellus, aided by C. Marius. The latter was by origin a knight from the once Volscian town of Arpinum, made fully Roman in 188. A 'new man', he had both military ability and connections with the business world, but chose, with support from the Metelli and other aristocratic families, to develop his military career into a political one. While serving with Metellus as a senior officer, he left after a quarrel to stand for the consulship of 107 and secured this by denouncing (somewhat unfairly) Metellus' methodical conduct of the war.

Marius was given the African command by plebiscite and took an army of volunteers, some of whom were veterans but others from among the landless, not normally allowed into the legions. Although Marius achieved good discipline in the army and some military success, he failed to pin down Jugurtha, but in 105 the latter was conveniently betrayed by the King of Mauretania to Marius' quaestor Sulla. Within a few months Marius was back in Rome, elected to an extraordinary second consulship in 104 in order to organise the defence of Italy against two Germanic peoples, the Cimbri and Teutones.

The subjection of Cisalpine Gaul, including Venetia, and the Dalmatian coast had required Rome to defend these areas against incursions from the peoples to the North. Moreover, in the late 120s she had led her armies beyond the Alps into Provence, in order to eliminate the threat to her ally Massilia from the Gauls there, and in the end subjected an area stretching as far north as Toulouse and Vienne in the Rhône valley (a colony was established at Narbonne). Then she suffered a series of military defeats at the hands of Celtic or Germanic armies – in 113, 109, 107 and, most calamitously, in 105 at Arausio in the Rhône valley.

Marius proceeded to remodel the Roman army and retrain it, removing the distinctions between the various ranks of infantry in the interest of simplicity and flexibility and encouraging the mobility of the army between engagements. It was not necessarily a better army than that which had defeated Hannibal and the Macedonians, but it was more suited to dealing with the onslaught of a mass of Celts or Germans. Successive extraordinary consulships left Marius still in command when the Teutones invaded again in 102, and they were defeated at Aquae Sextiae (Aix-en-Provence). This was followed by a more massive incursion of the Cimbri into northern Italy, defeated by Marius at Vercellae in 101. In these year the Romans also had to repress a second great slave revolt in Sicily and a surge of piracy in the East. At the height of his glory Marius achieved a sixth consulship in 100, a year when 'popular' politicians were once again ascendant.

In the previous decade there had already been several laws passed in the popular interest. Major priesthoods had been opened to a form of popular election. Trials and penalties for political crimes had been made more stringent: in particular a new court had been introduced by L. Appuleius Saturninus to deal with betraying the people by military failure or obstructing assemblies. After

Caepio in 106 put senators on to the juries of the *repetundae* court, C. Servilius Glaucia removed them again in 101. Moreover, Saturninus had legislated in 103 to settle Marian veterans on land in Africa.

In 100 Glaucia was praetor and Saturninus tribune, and we find a concerted attempt to construct a popular legislative programme, including intervention in foreign policy. In order to fight the Cimbri Marius must have recruited widely, even from the landless. Saturninus passed agrarian legislation on behalf of his veterans, the Italians included, exploiting the land seized by the Cimbri in northern Italy and sites in the provinces. He also revived the Gracchan grain law. The measures were forced through in face of violent opposition and alleged bad omens.

Marius' embarrassment at his allies' behaviour was aggravated when Glaucia illegally sought election to the consulship for 99 with the aid of further violence. After a decree similar to that used against Gaius Gracchus in 121, Marius became the defender of the Republic with an emergency militia: Glaucia, Saturninus and their friends were besieged, forced to surrender and then stoned to death with roof-tiles, while in theory under Marius' protection.

There is uncertainty about the fate of the legislation: in part at least it was ignored, not formally repealed, but within two years there was a statute that allowed the senate to decide that a law was invalid because it was passed through improper procedure. It is sometimes alleged that Marius invented the personal army. He certainly recruited the landless in 107 and probably in 104 onwards, when it was traditional in a military crisis, and he sought to reward them with land. However, it was Saturninus, not he, who was backed by the violence of his veterans, and he showed no desire yet to take over Rome with soldiers. Civil war was to be the product of the final crisis in Rome's relations with Italy.

In 95 feelings were exacerbated after a new measure against the usurpation of Roman citizenship. It is likely that this led Italian leaders – who, we are told, wished to be partners in the Roman empire, not subordinates – to concert plans for a possible secession. Then in 91 the tribune M. Livius Drusus (son of Gaius Gracchus' opponent) produced a package of measures that would have simultaneously restored senatorial authority in politics at Rome and united Italy under the leadership of men like himself. There were to be new land distributions, a new grain law, an enlarged senate, the return of senators to the juries of the criminal courts and the grant of Roman citizenship to all Italy.

Drusus hoped that by giving something to most sectors of the Roman population he could get enough support for the Italian bill. The knights were hostile to him, many senators suspicious and, though he had mass support from certain regions of Italy, Etruria was against him. He seems to have actually got his legislation through the assembly, but it was alleged that he had improperly tacked items together, and the senate voted to declare his legislation invalid. He himself was mysteriously murdered in the atrium of his house towards the end of the year and within a few months a Roman magistrate stumbled on a conspiracy in eastern Italy, thus precipitating the outbreak of an Italian rebellion – the War of the Allies or 'Social War'.

SEVEN

War and Unification in Italy

In the rebellion of 91 the Latins remained loyal to Rome, except for one colony in Apulia – Venusia. The insurgents were joined by all the Italian peoples, except the majority of the Etruscans and Umbrians. For the first time there was a confederation of Italians that transcended tribal loyalties. They established a capital with political institutions at Corfinium, renamed Italica, and issued coins with legends in Oscan and patriotic iconography – one showed the bull of Italy trampling on the wolf of Rome. The allied armies could not penetrate into Latium and threaten Rome. However, in Campania, although Roman territory, Oscan cities such as Pompeii joined the revolt. During the course of 90 the Romans forced a route through to the Adriatic in order to divide the revolt. Fighting was then concentrated in Picenum, especially round Asculum, and in western Samnium and Campania. Meanwhile, at Rome suspicion of Drusus' friends and others led to a special tribunal investigating those alleged to have collaborated in the revolt.

Heavy demands were made on Roman manpower. Because of the emergency time-served veterans and those without property were recruited; even freed slaves were used to garrison the coast. Immense demands were made too on the Roman treasury, as the massive coin issues of 90 BC show. It was, however, clear that military action was inadequate and later in the year legislation was passed conferring Roman citizenship on Italians who had not taken up arms or who had laid them down swiftly. This kept Etruria and Umbria as a whole out of the war.

In 89 the war was effectively decided. In the south Sulla recovered most of Campania and then took a series of towns in Samnium, while Cosconius was victorious in Apulia. In the north the Marsi were defeated, and at the end of the year the Picentine capital Asculum was taken by the consul Cn. Pompeius Strabo. There remained pockets of resistance in

Samnium and at Nola in Campania, and a more serious war in Lucania to be finished. Citizenship was in theory available for those who abandoned the Italian cause, but the new citizens were to be confined to only eight or ten tribes added to the existing thirty-five, thus limiting their voting power. Many Romans had died. Others had been bankrupted. A praetor who was making decrees favourable to debtors in 89 was lynched by a mob of creditors. In this fluid situation Rome's dominance of the eastern Mediterranean was shaken (and much of her income from there was lost), precipitating a crisis in Italy that in the long run matched the 'Social War'.

Mithridates VI Eupator of Pontus came from a dynasty in north-eastern Asia Minor that combined Greek language and culture with a blood line allegedly descending from the Achaemenids of Persia. The kingdom had been created amid the disintegration of Alexander the Great's empire. The homeland was rich agriculturally and had magnificent forests; it also had plentiful minerals, including iron, silver, lead and zinc. The dynasty had expanded its power in Asia Minor and round the Black Sea. Relations with Rome had been generally good. Mithridates V had helped Rome against Aristonicus and was rewarded with the grant of Phrygia, allegedly after bribery. After his death in 120, however, the Romans took it back. His son Mithridates VI was for some years kept from power, but then seized the throne from his mother. He first asserted Pontic influence north and west of the Black Sea, then expanded westwards in Asia Minor into Paphlagonia and Galatia, while maintaining a dynastic link with the royal house of Cappadocia. By about 100 BC he had his own son as king there.

In about 96 Sulla, as governor of Cilicia, used diplomatic pressure to install a Roman nominee in Cappadocia (he also had discussions with the new force in the Near East, the Parthians, on the River Euphrates), but after his departure this king was deposed by Mithridates. Nicomedes III of Bithynia had been intriguing with the Romans against Mithridates. When he died in 91, Mithridates expelled the successor recognised by Rome, Nicomedes IV, in favour of that king's brother. The next year a Roman embassy, headed by Manius Aquillius, backed by a small military force, persuaded Mithridates to give way both in Bithynia and Cappadocia, but it overreached when it urged Nicomedes IV to invade Pontus as a reprisal and a source of plunder.

Mithridates reacted with a full-scale attack on not only Bithynia but the Roman province of Asia and Rome's other allies. He met with little resistance (the exceptions were Rhodes, Lycia and some towns in Caria). Cities in general welcomed him as a liberator from Roman tax collectors and settlers: enormous numbers of Romans are said to have been massacred. In 88 Mithridates used his naval power (apart from his own fleet, he had an alliance with the pirates) to cross the Aegean and liberate Greece, while simultaneously invading Macedonia by land. Athens was brought over to his side by pro-Pontic tyrants (Mithridates' name appeared on Athenian coins); so did Sparta, Achaea and most of Boeotia, but northern Greece remained loyal to the Romans.

The disastrous news first reached Rome in late 89 and Sulla, as one of the consuls of 88, was assigned the Mithridatic War, though he was slow to set out because he wished to finish the siege of Nola. Marius, who had served successfully in the 'Social War' and had met Mithridates when in Asia Minor in the 90s, likewise coveted this command, probably hoping also for a seventh consulship. He allied himself with a vigorous tribune, P. Sulpicius Rufus, who was agitating in 88 for a fairer integration of the Italians in the voting system. Sulpicius could only pass his Italian legislation after violence, in the face of which Sulla retired from Rome to his army at Nola.

Now Sulpicius legislated to strip Sulla immediately of command of the army that was to fight Mithridates, and give this to Marius. Sulla persuaded his troops to defend his honour, suggesting that Marius might dismiss them as unreliable. So, when Marius' officers came to take command, they were stoned to death. Sulla straightway led his army on Rome. He perhaps pretended that as consul he was going to restore order, but the use of legions within the city boundary was against tradition. His own ambitions for a glorious and profitable campaign in Asia were shared by his troops and any scruples about killing their own countrymen had been weakened by the war against the allies.

The city had no regular troops and fell to Sulla amid desperate resistance from the plebs; Marius, Sulpicius and their leading partisans fled. Sulla immediately had them declared enemies to be killed on sight and rescinded Sulpicius' legislation. He proposed constitutional reforms that would have increased the size of the senate, given it a veto over legislation, and abolished assemblies based on the tribes, leaving only the military assembly. These drastically reactionary reforms did not survive long.

In 87 Sulla left for Greece with his army. One of the new consuls, however, L. Cornelius Cinna, tried to revive Sulpicius' legislation about the Italians, quarrelling with his colleague Octavius. Violence broke out and Cinna, imitating Sulla, went to Nola and took over the army there. He now marched on Rome with Italian support. Sulpicius had been found and killed when in hiding, but Marius had escaped to Africa, where his veterans were. He now returned on Cinna's invitation and joined him with an army raised in Etruria.

Meanwhile, Pompeius Strabo, who had remained in command of the Roman army occupying Picenum, had not permitted the other consul of 88, Pompeius Rufus, to take over this army but instigated his troops to kill Rufus. He was summoned by Octavius to protect Rome, as was Q. Metellus, the commander of the army in Samnium. There was more serious resistance than in 88, but Pompeius Strabo died of disease, Metellus kept his distance, and eventually, after cutting off its supplies and promising freedom to the slaves, Marius and Cinna entered Rome by agreement.

In spite of Cinna's promises of moderation there was a massacre of senators and knights at Marius' instigation and the newly liberated slaves took the opportunity to loot and kill. Sulla himself was declared a public enemy. Marius was elected to his seventh consulship, with Cinna as his colleague, for 86, but died after holding office for thirteen days. Sulla's constitutional changes were evidently repealed and the Republic apparently returned to normal, except that the consulships were dominated by two leading Marians, Cinna and Cn. Papirius Carbo. The shortage of cash created by civil war (when much was hoarded and often lost) was remedied by a massive remission of debts. There was also peace in Italy for a while: the remaining Samnites were reconciled by the offer of citizenship, the war in south Italy was brought to an end. Sulpicius' proposals about the voting of new citizens were also revived, though not until 84. A number of Sullan sympathisers, however, either went into hiding or joined Sulla in Greece.

Sulla had marched rapidly through Greece from the North in 87 and besieged the rich prize of

Athens and its port Piraeus. Athens fell on 1 March 86 and the Piraeus shortly afterwards. Aristion and other political leaders were killed and the city looted. Sulla then performed his greatest military exploits by defeating two successive Pontic armies in Boeotia – at Chaeronea and Orchomenus – in spite of inferior numbers.

Meanwhile, a Marian army under the replacement consul of 86, Valerius Flaccus, had advanced through Macedonia and crossed the Bosphorus into Asia Minor. There Flaccus was murdered by his troops with the encouragement of his deputy, Flavius Fimbria, but in 85 the latter carried on an effective campaign of taking back cities from Mithridates, whose brutal treatment of some of his new subjects had undermined his initial popularity. Lucullus had meanwhile collected a fleet for Sulla from Rome's allies and they advanced to the Hellespont, where they concluded an agreement with Mithridates. Mithridates was to surrender all the territory acquired in the war and his control of Paphlagonia, Galatia and Cappadocia; he was to hand over seventy warships, grain and an indemnity in money; in return his control of his former empire was to be recognised. Sulla now turned against Fimbria, defeated him and forced him to suicide. Of the liberated cities of Asia, the few that had resisted Mithridates were rewarded with privileges, the rest were subjected to a huge indemnity and had to provide money and lodging for Sulla's soldiers. Following their Asiatic holiday, these were transported back to Greece in 84 BC, prior to an invasion of Italy the next year.

Though Sulla offered terms, the Marian leaders could not approve his return at the head of an army. So he arrived at Brindisi in 83 as an enemy. Cinna had been killed by his own soldiers in 84. Sulla fought his way into Campania; one consul confronted him there, but his men were persuaded to desert. Sulla was joined by a number of supporters, including the young Pompey, Pompeius Strabo's son, with a private army. He also sought to conciliate the Italians.

The following year he himself advanced on Rome while other armies put pressure on the Marian forces concentrated in Etruria. Victorious near Rome, Sulla penned up Marius' son in Praeneste and forced the Marians to leave the city. Campaigning continued through the year until an attempt was made to relieve the young Marius in

Praeneste with the aid of a large levy of Samnites. The Marian force was defeated with immense casualties outside Rome by the Colline Gate on 1 November. Their war effort now collapsed and their leaders were pursued to the provinces and killed, with the exception of Q. Sertorius who had gone to Spain.

On his return to Rome Sulla's first political moves were to get himself appointed dictator for re-establishing constitutional government and to legitimise proscriptions – a form of political cleansing, whereby Marian sympathisers were marked down for execution and confiscation of property – this in addition to the numbers killed in the aftermath of victory. Constitutional reform included an increase in the number of senators – who were now to be drawn exclusively from ex-magistrates and to have a monopoly of the criminal tribunals – an increase in numbers of magistrates, and a curtailment of the powers of tribunes: the latter were to be barred from further office and stripped of their power to legislate and to prosecute in an assembly. The statutes governing the criminal courts were revised: in particular the rules affecting governors of provinces were made stricter.

Although the grant of citizenship to Italians was not revoked in principle, certain defeated enemies were deprived of rights, their land being confiscated for the Roman people. These were the areas where Sulla settled his soldiers, especially Etruria and Campania: the Oscan city of Pompeii now became a colony of Sulla's veterans. By 79 Sulla was in retirement; the next year he was dead of disease. His partisans were now dominant in the senate and among the knights; they had also enriched themselves in the proscriptions. However, these had generated such disgust that Sulla's name was a bogey word in the years that followed.

EIGHT

The Breakdown of the Republic

For a decade after Sulla's victory the civil war smouldered, while in the East there was unfinished business. At home the plebs did not tamely acquiesce in the loss of political rights through Sulla's constitution. Yet Sulla's new aristocracy contributed to their problems by arrogance and corruption. Sulla was not yet dead when Marcus Lepidus, consul in 78, advocated the rescinding of Sulla's confiscations of Italian land and the renewal of distributions of cheap grain in the city, which Sulla had abolished. Sent to quell an uprising in Etruria, he put himself at the head of the insurgents, but was defeated the following year by Catulus with the aid of Pompey. The latter, after helping in Italy in 83–2, had recovered Sicily and Africa for Sulla. He still was too young for any major magistracy in 77, when after being deputed to be Catulus' officer, he defeated Marian remnants in Cisalpine Gaul. He was then sent West to deal with a rebellion in Transalpine Gaul and afterwards to join Metellus Pius in suppressing the Marian survivor Sertorius.

Sertorius had gone to Spain in 82. When the Marian cause collapsed in Italy, he withdrew temporarily to Mauretania (Morocco), but by 80 had returned and established himself in Lusitania (Portugal). His power spread to southern Spain and thence over much of the peninsula. There he created a miniature of the Roman state from Marian refugees and settlers. He also raised many Spaniards to the status of Romans by education and Roman military training, inspiring among them immense personal devotion. For many years the Roman commanders made little permanent impression on his power: every year they were compelled to winter their armies outside the peninsula.

In the East the Romans increased their grip on central Asia Minor but, unwisely, they refused to give Mithridates a formal treaty. So, when in 75 Nicomedes IV of Bithynia died and left his kingdom to Rome,

Mithridates took the opportunity to invade Bithynia and Asia once more. The next year the consuls Lucullus and Cotta were sent against him amid a scandal regarding the corruption surrounding provincial appointments (they depended on a 'broker's' mistress). Meanwhile, the pirates flourished. Their strongholds in Cilicia and Crete were untouched and they ranged the whole Mediterranean: when Sertorius sought an alliance with Mithridates, his ambassadors were conveyed on their ships. The commander commissioned to deal with the problem in 74, M. Antonius, proved ineffective.

At Rome piracy interrupted the corn supply and exacerbated plebeian unrest. As a sop, a law was passed in 75 restoring the right of tribunes to seek further office, thus opening the magistracy again to potential high-fliers, and in 73 grain distributions were restored for a section of the city population. Italy was dominated by the Sullan sympathisers, who had bought land in the proscriptions and now preyed on each other with assassinations and battles between their slave gangs. However, in 73 the slaves began to fight for themselves. A group of gladiators led by Spartacus, Crixus and Oenomaus broke out of a training school in Capua and gathered widespread support from the slaves and free herdsmen on the big estates in south Italy. They defeated several regular Roman armies before finally succumbing to Marcus Crassus in 71.

Meanwhile, Metellus and Pompey had returned after ending the rebellion in Spain. Sertorius had been assassinated by leading Romans for allegedly sacrificing military efficiency to high living, and his successor Perperna could not match his skills. There was also better news for Rome from the East. In spite of Mithridates' early success by sea, Lucullus had prevented him establishing himself securely on land in western Bithynia; the Pontic fleets were then driven from the approaches to the Black Sea and Lucullus invaded Pontus itself, defeating Mithridates at Cabeira.

When Pompey returned, he stood for the consulship of 70 with Crassus in spite of having held none of the preliminary magistracies. Unusually, the candidates had a programme: they promised to restore the powers of the tribunes and reform the corruption of the courts. Pompey was exempted from the laws and the pair was elected in an assembly full of their own soldiers. Sulla's former partisans felt that it was better to give way to popular pressure: the tribunate was an insurance against corruption in the aristocracy. This was currently epitomised by Gaius Verres, a governor who had ruthlessly plundered and exploited Sicily for three years in the expectation of bribing a senatorial jury with the proceeds. In 70 a consular law duly restored their former powers to the tribunes, while jury service was entrusted to panels drawn from not only senators but knights and other wealthy non-senators. Verres was condemned by one of the last senatorial juries thanks to the vigorous advocacy of Marcus Tullius Cicero – another 'new man' from Arpinum who was pursuing a political career at Rome through forensic success rather than soldiering. Censors were also elected for the first time for many years. They enrolled a great number of Italians, whose formal recognition as Romans had hitherto been blocked, and expelled from the senate sixty-four unworthy men.

In 67 tribunes once again were very active. In the interval Lucullus had occupied Pontus and then tried to pursue Mithridates when he took refuge with Tigranes, King of Armenia, a Parthian vassal. In so doing he neglected Asia Minor and Mithridates returned to secure a considerable victory over the Roman forces there, forcing Lucullus to leave Armenia. Lucullus' provinces were successively transferred to other commanders, the last by the tribune Gabinius in 67. Gabinius also sought a final solution to the pirate problem by proposing an immense command for a single commander. His power was to extend for three years over all the Mediterranean and up to 50 miles inland; he was to have 15 lieutenants, at least 270 ships, 20 legions, 4,000 cavalry and the right to use public money wherever it was stored in the empire. This was approved in the face of senatorial opposition and the command conferred on Pompey. In the same year Gabinius and Cornelius sponsored plebiscites aimed at restricting the corruption of magistrates and senators and stimulated a consular bill against electoral bribery.

Pompey was immensely successful. Within weeks the pirates were exterminated from the West and in three months from the whole Mediterranean. It remained to besiege their strongholds in Crete and Cilicia. Meanwhile, neither Lucullus through weakness nor his successor through timidity were fighting Mithridates. In consequence, a tribune of 66, Manilius, proposed the transfer of the commands in Cilicia, Bithynia and the Mithridatic War to Pompey on terms similar to those in Gabinius' law: he was in addition to have the power to undertake new wars and make alliances.

Pompey rapidly defeated Mithridates at Dasteira and forced him to flee northwards through the Caucasus, from which he eventually reached refuge in the Crimea. Tigranes of Armenia, who had in the eighties BC taken over the remnants of the Syrian empire, put himself in Pompey's hands and was allowed to retain his original kingdom but not his recent gains. Pompey campaigned in the Caucasus and the Iberi and Albani there became Roman allies. In 64 he proceeded to organise both Bithynia-Pontus and Syria as a provinces, while intervening in Judaea to instal his own nominee Hyrcanus as high priest (the territory beyond the Euphrates was largely ceded to Parthia).

In 63 Mithridates himself was finally killed or forced to suicide in his Crimean stronghold in a *coup d'état* by his son Pharnaces, who then submitted to Pompey. Before Pompey returned to Rome in 62, he had reorganised the East with four provinces – Asia, Cilicia, Bithynia-Pontus and Syria – intertwined with a large number of allied kingdoms, ranging from

Cappadocia to small city states like Apamea and Emesa. A great number of Eastern rulers were deeply, and literally, in his debt.

At Rome during this period some significant measures were mooted. In 65, Crassus proposed to annex Egypt, following the now twenty-year-old will of Ptolemy Alexander I, but others did not wish so much wealth and potential power to fall into his hands. Crassus also backed a major land bill in 63, Cicero's consulship, designed to find room for veteran soldiers in Italy at the cost of selling existing public land, mainly abroad. Cicero opposed both bills through his suspicions of those who were to be commissioners and his fundamental opposition to land redistribution. Crassus' junior associate in these proposals was C. Iulius Caesar, a patrician and former Marian. He was making a name for himself as a popular politician, supporting the Gabinian law, reviving memories of Marius and encouraging prosecutions of agents of the Sullan proscriptions.

Political alignments were, however, confused by the career of Catiline (L. Sergius Catilina). He was patrician and a former henchman of Sulla, who was accused in the recovery court of extortion when governor of Africa. Although acquitted, his bid for the consulship was delayed from 66 to 64, when he became a competitor of Cicero's, but was apparently backed by Crassus and Caesar. He was attacked for planning to assassinate senators and using violence to obstruct trials in 66–5 and his candidacy failed. When Cicero was consul, he once again was a candidate with a programme of cancelling debts, backed by discontented peasants from Etruria who were landless or in debt. After this candidacy failed, the peasants broke out into rebellion and he, after concerting a conspiracy aimed at a *coup d'état* in Rome, was forced to flee from the city, when news of this was leaked to Cicero by Crassus and others.

The conspirators at Rome were detected and their leaders executed after a famous debate in the senate on 5 December 63; soon afterwards Catiline was killed at the head of the peasant army in Etruria. Cicero was hailed as the saviour of his country. The conspiracy exposed aristocratic nervousness about the plebs of Rome, vastly increased by liberated slaves, often of foreign origin, and by other immigrants. They lived in appalling conditions and were easily stimulated to violence. It also highlighted the debts among the aristocracy, aggravated by the shortage of cash caused by financial uncertainty in the East and their own reckless spending in the pursuit of status and high office.

On his return from the East Pompey found his fame eclipsed by a religious scandal. A young patrician, Publius Clodius, was accused of sacrilege for surreptitiously joining a ceremony reserved for women, held in Caesar's house. He was acquitted amid allegations that the jury was bribed, in spite of Cicero giving evidence against him. Pompey eventually celebrated a two-day triumph in September 61. He wished to settle his veterans on the land but found it difficult to get an appropriate bill passed; he also wanted ratification of his Eastern settlement, but this had aroused suspicions of graft and was obstructed in the senate by Lucullus' relative Cato. Cato also opposed an attempt by the tax collectors in Asia to get partial remission of what they owed the treasury under their contract but had found difficult to collect through the financial exhaustion of the province.

Caesar, meanwhile, had been praetor and governed Spain. He returned to seek the consulship of 59. Before he entered office he had organised a coalition with Pompey and Crassus. The first result of this was an agrarian bill for Pompey's veterans, which Caesar forced through by violence in face of obstruction by tribunes and the announcement of evil omens. After the senate declined to declare this invalid, Caesar, with the help of the tribune Vatinius, passed further bills. One ratified Pompey's settlement, another secured the tax collectors their remission, a third gave recognition to the King of Egypt in return for a large bribe; there was a further agrarian bill, offering land to the plebs of Rome in Campania, and Caesar obtained for himself a five-year command in Cisalpine Gaul and Illyricum.

This command was enlarged by the senate on Pompey's proposal to include Transalpine Gaul. Rome's province and allies there had come under threat from two quarters. The Helvetii in present-day Switzerland wished to migrate to the Bay of Biscay, while the German chief Ariovistus was seeking to obtain overlordship of the Gallic peoples north of the province. A great opportunity lay before Caesar; Pompey for his part received Caesar's only daughter in marriage, a seal of their political alliance. The three dynasts also secured for Clodius, who had been building up support among the city plebs, transfer to plebeian status, so permitting him to be elected tribune.

105

As tribune in 58 Clodius embarked on a popular programme, simultaneously paying off old scores. Grain distributions had been extended by Cato in 62 to the whole citizen population of Rome; Clodius now made these free of charge. He also legalised the 'colleges', i.e. the associations among the plebs based on trade, location and religious cult, and exploited them for systematic violence (the reason why they had been dissolved earlier). Other laws of his made it more difficult to use religious obstruction against political acts, altered the allocation of the provinces to the benefit of the consuls and appointed Cato to take possession of Cyprus for the benefit of the Roman people, so removing him from Rome. Cicero, however, was made to pay for his attacks on Clodius. A law provided for the immediate banishment of anyone who had executed a citizen without trial (technically true of Cicero's action in 63, since the senate was no court) and when Cicero eventually left, Clodius confiscated his property and turned his house into a shrine of Liberty.

Clodius now turned on Pompey, harassing him and humiliating him. Even when he left office, he was master of the streets of Rome until Cicero's friends collected gangs under Milo and Sestius to oppose him. Pompey got his revenge when Cicero's return was voted through in August 57 and, owing to a failure in supplies, Pompey received a command over grain provision. However, Clodius' gangs were still active and Pompey was harassed politically by enemies in the senate until May 56 when a new coalition was formed.

After defeating the Helvetii and Ariovistus, Caesar interpreted his task in Gaul as the subjection of all the territory west of the Rhine. He had largely completed this when he met Crassus, Pompey and many other senators in north Italy. It was agreed that Pompey and Crassus should become consuls in 55 and then all three should have major provincial commands, that Clodius should help rather than harass Pompey and that Cicero should be persuaded to speak in support of the agreement. After violence and political chicanery Pompey and Crassus were duly elected in early 55. They then legislated that Caesar's commands should be extended for five years, while a tribune Trebonius provided that Crassus should govern Syria and Pompey the Spanish provinces in his absence for the same period. The coalition thus would hold between them most of the important provinces and upwards of twenty legions.

Crassus had ambitions to match his partners' military glory by a profitable campaign against Parthia. He declared war on a flimsy pretext, but his invasion was indecisive and his expected allies unreliable. His army was cut to pieces by Parthian cavalry and mounted archers on the plain of Carrhae in Mesopotamia in 53, only a small section escaping to Syria under C. Cassius (the later assassin of Caesar). Caesar sought good publicity by crossing the Rhine in 55 to engage the Germans and the 'Ocean' in 55 and 54 to fight in south-east Britain, before being tied down by a series of Gallic revolts that lasted from the autumn of 54 until summer 51.

Pompey stayed on the outskirts of Rome, hoping for an extraordinary magistracy that would allow him to reform matters in the city, as a plethora of corruption and violence brought the magistracies into disrepute. At the beginning of 52 Milo was a candidate in the delayed elections for the consulship, while Clodius was a candidate for the praetorship with a programme of improved political status for former slaves. In a brawl between their armed entourages on the Appian Way Milo had his men kill Clodius. This produced uproar in the city as the plebs mourned their hero. The violence grew so bad that Pompey was first asked to use his soldiers to restore order and then was elected sole consul. Milo and others were condemned for violence by a special tribunal; the law on electoral corruption was made more effective, and there was legislation separating magistracies at home from command overseas (so that the latter should not finance expenditure on obtaining the former).

Pompey himself, nonetheless, at the end of his consulship undertook a new term of office in Spain, while remaining as before in his villa overlooking Rome. He was now the favourite of the leading senators, while his connection with Caesar had been weakened by the death of his wife Julia in childbirth in 54. He wished to maintain his position as the leading man in the Roman Republic, but the return of Caesar threatened this, especially if the latter maintained his appetite for radical measures.

Caesar was now nearing the end of his ten-year commands, though precisely when they began and ended was a matter of some confusion. He wished to return to be consul a second time in 48 and then perhaps take on the Parthians, who by now had invaded Syria. His problem was that his old enemies, now Pompey's friends, would take any opportunity to prosecute him if he was without a magistracy. He planned to exploit a law of 52 allowing him to stand for the consulship in his absence and stay with his army until the last moment. From mid-51 to the first week in 49 there was increasing pressure from the senate and Pompey for Caesar to give up his army (Caesar's last offer was to retain Cisalpine Gaul with one or two legions). Then the senate voted for him to return and for his army to be disbanded by a fixed date. Two tribunes vetoed this, but they withdrew under threats; Pompey's troops occupied the city, and on 7 January the emergency decree was passed urging the consuls to defend the Republic. When the news reached Caesar, he crossed the Rubicon into Italy with the vanguard of his army.

So began twenty years of civil war, dictatorship, assassination and confiscation. Pompey was defeated in Greece by Caesar in 48, his sons and supporters in Africa and Spain in 46–5. The victorious Caesar, proclaimed perpetual dictator, was killed by opponents of tyranny on 15 March 44, thus precipitating a new struggle for power. The forms of the Republic continued – as they did even under the emperors – but force, not law, was the ultimate criterion and political liberty was rarely seen, even though Caesar's assassins hoped it would return more securely.

When in the time of Caesar Augustus, Caesar's adopted son and his successor, explanations for the breakdown were sought, the usual answers were moral corruption and the ambition of great men. Some argued that the size of the empire was too great for any form of collective rule: efficiency and the avoidance of faction required the rule of one man: this also reduced the need for policies calculated to win popular approval. For over a millennium there were to be Roman emperors, first at Rome and later in Constantinople. It was only when the city states of medieval Europe were seeking to shake off the dominance of the Church and their secular potentates that the Roman Republic was revived as an example and had in the long run a major influence on our political thought.

Further Reading

GENERAL

Beard, M., North, J. and Price, S. *Religions of Rome: Volume I: A History*, Cambridge, 1998

Brunt, P.A. *Italian Manpower*, Oxford, 1971

Claridge, A. *Rome (Oxford Archaeological Guides)*, Oxford, 1998

Cornell, T. and Matthews, J. *Atlas of the Roman World*, London, 1982

Crawford, M. *Coinage and Money under the Roman Republic*, London, 1985

——. *The Roman Republic*, second edn, London, 1992

Crook, J.A. *Law and Life of Rome*, London, 1967

Cunliffe, B. *Greeks, Romans and Barbarians*, London, 1988

David, J.-M. *The Roman Conquest of Italy*, trans. Antonia Nevill, Oxford, 1997

Frank, T. *Economic Survey of Ancient Rome*, vol. I, Baltimore, 1933

Gardner, J.E. *Women in Roman Law and Society*, London, 1986

Gelzer, M. *The Roman Nobility*, trans. R. Seager, Oxford, 1969

Harris, W.V. *War and Imperialism in Republican Rome 327–70 BC*, Oxford, 1979

Hopkins, K. *Conquerors and Slaves*, Cambridge, 1978

——. *Death and Renewal*, Cambridge, 1983

Lintott, A. *Imperium Romanum. Politics and Administration*, London, 1993

——. *The Constitution of the Roman Republic*, Oxford, 1999

——. *Violence in Republican Rome*, second edn, Oxford, 1999

112

Nicolet, C. *The World of the Citizen in Republican Rome*, trans. P.S. Falla, London, 1980

Nippel, W. *Public Order in Ancient Rome*, Cambridge, 1995

Rawson, E. *Intellectual Life in the Roman Republic*, London, 1985

Richardson, J.S. *The Romans in Spain*, Oxford, 1996

Sherwin White, A.N. *Roman Foreign Policy in the East*, London, 1984

THE EARLY AND MIDDLE REPUBLIC

Cornell, T.J. *The Beginnings of Rome 753–263 BC*, London, 1995

Cambridge Ancient History, second edn, vols: VII.2, *The Rise of Rome to 220 BC*, ed. F.W. Walbank, A.E. Astin, M.W. Frederiksen, R.M. Ogilvie, 1989; VIII, *Rome and the Mediterranean to 133 BC*, ed. A.E. Astin, F.W. Walbank, M.W. Frederiksen, R.M. Ogilvie, 1989

Gruen, E.S. *The Hellenistic World and the Coming of Rome*, 2 vols, Berkeley and Los Angeles, 1984

Lancel, S. *Hannibal*, trans. Antonia Nevill, Oxford, 1998

——. *Carthage. A History*, trans. Antonia Nevill, Oxford, 1995

Lazenby, J.F. *The First Punic War*, London, 1996

——. *Hannibal's War. A Military History of the Second Punic War*, Warminster, 1978

Scullard, H.H. *A History of the Roman World 753–146 BC*, fourth edn, London, 1980

Walbank, F.W. *Polybius*, Berkeley and Los Angeles, 1972

THE LATE REPUBLIC

Badian, E. *Roman Imperialism in the Late Republic*, second edn, Oxford, 1968

Beard, M. and Crawford, M. *Rome in the Late Republic. Problems and Interpretations*, London, 1985

Brunt, P.A. *The Fall of the Roman Republic*, Oxford, 1988

Cambridge Ancient History, second edn, vol. IX, *The Last Age of the Roman Republic 146–43 BC*, ed. J.A. Crook, A. Lintott, E. Rawson, 1994

Gruen, E.S. *The Last Generation of the Roman Republic*, Berkeley and Los Angeles, 1974

Millar, F. *The Crowd in Rome in the late Republic*, Ann Arbor, 1998

Scullard, H.H. *From the Gracchi to Nero*, fifth edn, London, 1982 (1988)

Seager, R. *Pompey: A Political Biography*, Oxford, 1979

Stockton, D. *Cicero: A Political Biography*, Oxford, 1971

——. *The Gracchi*, Oxford, 1979

Syme, Sir R. *The Roman Revolution*, Oxford, 1939

Taylor, L.R. *Party Politics in the Age of Caesar*, Berkeley and Los Angeles, 1949

The *Cambridge Ancient History* provides both narrative and analytical chapters. Cornell and the two works of Scullard provide primarily narrative histories of their respective periods. Rome's imperial growth can be studied both in theory and in detail in the works of Badian, Cunliffe, David, Gruen (1984), Harris, Lintott (1993), Richardson and Sherwin White, Cunliffe and Richardson providing accounts of Roman activity in the West, while Gruen and Sherwin White deal with the East. Rome's relations with Carthage and the Punic Wars are treated by Lancel and Lazenby. The economic crisis is discussed in both works of Brunt and in that of Hopkins (1978); the aristocracy in Gelzer (1969) and Hopkins (1983) – the latter also deals with gladiators and Roman attitudes to death. Political violence is treated by Lintott (1999), Nippel (1995), and Millar (1998) (the first two books also deal more generally with the place of violence in society). The titles of the other books are, I hope, self-explanatory.

Index

All general entries refer to Rome/Roman Republic unless otherwise indicated.